THE
SEVEN
POWERS OF
SUCCESS

THE
SEVEN
POWERS OF
SUCCESS

CHARLES MARSHALL

HARVEST HOUSE PUBLISHERS
EUGENE, OREGON

Charles Marshall is represented by MacGregor Literary, Inc. of Hillsboro, Oregon.

This book contains stories in which people's names and some details of their situations have been changed in order to protect their identity.

Cover by Left Coast Design, Portland, Oregon

Back cover author photo © Jennifer Stalcup

THE SEVEN POWERS OF SUCCESS
Copyright © 2013 by Charles Marshall
Published by Harvest House Publishers
Eugene, Oregon 97402
www.harvesthousepublishers.com

Library of Congress Cataloging-in-Publication Data
Marshall, Charles W. (Charles Wesley)
The seven powers of success / Charles Marshall.
   pages cm
ISBN 978-0-7369-5233-0 (pbk.)
ISBN 978-0-7369-5234-7 (eBook)
1. Success. 2. Success in business. 3. Success—Religious aspects. 4. Success in business—Religious aspects. I. Title.
BF637.S8M289 2013
248.4—dc23

2012044767

Printed in the United States of America

13 14 15 16 17 18 19 20 21 / BP-CD / 10 9 8 7 6 5 4 3 2 1

To Faith and Wesley
You are my treasure.

CONTENTS

Introduction

Why are some people successful and not others? Why is it that some people seem to effortlessly glide through life while others are mired in dysfunction, heartache, poverty, and pain? Is it that some people are luckier and get all the breaks? Is it that some people have God's blessings and others don't? Or could it be that our whole system is corrupt and makes it impossible for anyone to rise above their station?

People blame their situation on God, the economy, their upbringing, their spouse, their family, or lack of opportunity, but none of these things are responsible for one's success. The only factor that determines whether people are successful is whether they apply the Seven Powers of Success.

Early in 2010, I got a call from a reporter of a large metropolitan newspaper. He had been given an assignment by his editor to do an article about how motivational speakers were going out of business because of the recession. After speaking with him for a few minutes, I learned that he wasn't calling me to research the story or check his facts. All he wanted was to get a couple of quotes from me to support his story. He told me he had already spoken with a couple of other speakers and come away with the dire news that the professional speaking industry was in deep trouble.

He asked me what I thought about the subject, and I told him I was having one my best years ever. When he asked me why things were going so well, I told him that in regard to my goals, my dreams, and my vision, I don't believe in backing up, backing down, or backing off. He seemed a bit put off with my answer, and I could tell this wasn't the story he came to get. He got off the phone pretty quickly afterward, and a few days later the story appeared without my comments. Go figure.

I got another call a few days later from a friend who told me that he had lost his job six months earlier. He said that he had done everything in his power to get a job but was coming up empty. There were just no jobs to be had in his field. To make matters worse, he felt that he had been abandoned by God. It was God's job to take care of him, and God had dropped the ball. He reasoned that if God wasn't providing for him, then either God wasn't so loving after all or there must not be any God.

I didn't blame my friend for his faith struggle. I've been through a few hard times myself. For the longest time in my life, I was a stranger to any kind of success—relational, financial, emotional, or spiritual. The first time I really became aware of differences between the successful and the unsuccessful was in junior high school. I may not have been the biggest loser in my class, but I was close to it. The fact that my family was dirt poor didn't help my social status at all.

At the age where kids are suddenly becoming aware of so much, including what one another is wearing, I was sporting hand-me-down clothes—from my older sisters. You may think I'm kidding, but my older brother had moved away from home by that time, so the only hand-me-downs that were available for me were from my older sisters. Fortunately, I'm not talking sundresses and high heels, but there were plenty instances when I wore my older sisters' crew-neck pullovers, and once, at my mother's insistence, I even tried wearing my sister's light print jeans.

"Nobody will even notice!" my mother insisted.

They did notice, and…well, let's just say I know firsthand that getting caught wearing your sister's pants will not make you more popular at school. At least not the good kind of popular.

On the rare occasion when I did get new clothes, they were always purchased at Kmart. "Attention Kmart shoppers! We are now running a special on dorky middle-school boys' clothing on aisle three!"

Mom would practically bolt down the aisle.

Everything a nerd could want: flimsy jeans with bright yellow outer-stitching that were two sizes too short, polyester print shirts, and Adidas knock-off tennis shoes that were made out of plastic.

That's right. Plastic. I kid you not. After two weeks on the playground, your tennis shoes were cracking like an old garden hose. You couldn't fix them because the duct tape just peeled right off.

I moved away from home six months after I graduated from high school. My first apartment cost $100 a month and was advertised as a "cozy, one-bedroom efficiency apartment located conveniently next to the university." Sounds lovely, doesn't it? The truth of the matter was that someone had sliced up a dilapidated old house into six or seven "efficiency" apartments and then rented them to college students. One crack where the floor met the wall was so big you could see straight through to the crawl space underneath the house. On cold nights I turned the gas space heater all the way up, but it barely touched the cold, so I also turned on the electric stove and oven. I remember waking up on chilly mornings with the thermometer reading in the upper forties or lower fifties inside my apartment.

25 to 30 Years Later

My memories from my recent past look a little bit different.

I remember doing a book signing in Orlando in 2008. A line of people waiting to get an autographed copy of my book—a collection of humorous essays titled *I'm Not Crazy, but I Might Be a Carrier*—stretches around the corner and out of sight. My wife and two young children stand off to my left, waiting patiently for more than two hours as I sign books and connect with all of the people standing in line. The time flashes by, and at the end of it, I feel like I've been to a great party—worn out but happy.

I also remember recording my second full-length comedy video the previous year. At the end of my performance I walk off stage and the crowd leaps to its feet and explodes in applause. I walk back out on stage and do my encore. I remember thinking at that moment that I really love this job. I get to travel all over the country speaking to people, laughing with them, and encouraging them to live successful lives. What could be better?

Not long after recording my video, I walk into a retail store and see my products on the shelves. My wife insists on taking a picture of me posing beside my book on the shelf of a major retailer. I'm wearing a goofy smile and pointing at my book. It's corny, but somehow I don't care.

My most treasured memories include times when people have come up to me after I've spoken and mention that they've been touched by my program. It's not unusual for people to approach me at the back of the room after I've finished my program and tell me they haven't laughed that much in years. Or sometimes people share their deeply personal stories about struggles they are going through, such as an illness or the loss of a loved one.

I'm always honored whenever this happens. I like to think that maybe folks recognize a kindred spirit, someone who has been through difficult times, just as they have. It's important to me that people know that what they see of me now—a guy traveling all over the place, laughing and encouraging folks—is only half the story, that the beginning of my tale looked rather bleak before it turned around.

After people hear the beginning, the next thing they want to know is how the story happened to change for the better. How does a poor, friendless, bullied, loser of a kid become one of the top humorous motivational speakers in the country? How does the same kid who had the wrong clothes, the wrong look, the wrong everything end up speaking to Fortune 100 and 500 companies? How can a person who was so mired in poverty, rejection, and failure create a motivational resources company that has continued to grow and prosper in one of the toughest economies in modern history?

Transition

When I was struggling in school, I sometimes stared out the window, daydreaming about becoming a world-famous rock star. One day things would be different. One day the loneliness and torture would end. One day I would be respected and admired.

For years I dreamed. And that's all it was for a long time—a dream, a fantasy. I didn't realize that success in life has rules, that just like any other natural law, success can be cataloged, defined, and described. I really believed that life was at least a little bit like a fairy tale, and I hoped that something wonderful would happen for me one day.

Everything I saw in the media confirmed this belief. In movies, couples somehow found their way together, heroes somehow defeated the villains, and everything somehow worked out for the protagonist in the end. In sports, when a last-place team came from way behind and seemed to achieve overnight success, the result was always referred to as a Cinderella story. And when music stars were interviewed, they always talked as if they were just hanging out, doing their thing, when they were almost magically discovered.

Yes, it was truly a magical world, I believed—except for the fact that none of those fairy tales seemed to include me. Gradually it began to dawn on me that in order to see any success in my life, I would have to adopt a different belief system. After a while, slowly but surely, things began to turn around for me as I applied these new lessons in my life. I began to write down the lessons I learned and communicate them to the people I found myself in front of.

Origin of the Seven Powers

I wrote my first book, *Shattering the Glass Slipper: Destroying Fairy-Tale Thinking Before It Destroys You*, in the summer of 2002. My wife and I had our first child the previous winter, and I had been thinking about how I didn't want my daughter to grow up believing life was a fairy tale. As our family grew, I knew I wanted to communicate to all my children the principles of success that had taken me so long to learn.

In *Shattering the Glass Slipper*, I show the dangers of fairy-tale thinking and propose an alternative philosophy called the Seven Powers of Success, which, if harnessed, developed, and applied, can create great success in our lives.

Over the years since I first wrote about the Seven Powers, I've spoken about them in corporations, associations, churches, and civic groups many times, and I've noticed that people were intensely interested in hearing more about them. I discovered that there are a great number of people out there who are just as interested in hearing about the Seven Powers as I am in talking about them.

As I have spoken about these principles over the years, I have continued to expand these concepts and gather stories to illustrate them, and I have included many of those ideas and stories in this book. I hope you will use the principles in this book to explore your possibilities and achieve your potential.

Somebody once asked me if I believe that everyone is destined to become successful. It might surprise you to know that I do not. I do, however, believe that although everyone is not *destined* for success, everyone is *designed* for it. But it is up to each of us to see that process through and decide for ourselves what level of achievement we are capable of reaching.

What about you? What do you think you might be able to do if given the right tools? How much do you think you could accomplish if you were empowered with the correct mind-set? I think it's time for you to find out.

The Nature of Success

I'm not a big fan of basset hounds. Some people love them, but I'm not one of those people.

I adopted a seven-month-old basset hound named Hannah from my next-door neighbor a few years after I got married. She needed a home, and I wanted a dog. The thing I discovered about basset hounds in general, and this dog in particular, is that they're very needy, and more important, they're very vocal about their needs.

Hannah was an outside dog for the most part, and soon after I got her, she developed the habit of sitting at my backdoor near meal-time, whining and whimpering until it was time to eat. This went on day after day, each day starting a bit earlier, until she was spending the greater part of the afternoon sitting at my backdoor, whining.

After about a week, I'd had enough. I finally decided something needed to be done, but not really knowing what to do, I did the first thing that came to mind. I went outside and ordered Hannah into her doghouse until it was time to feed her.

I don't know what outcome I expected, but I can tell you what I got. The lesson that Hannah took away from this experience was that if she wanted to eat, she needed to go sit in her doghouse. So from then on, about 30 minutes before mealtime, she would stand in the doorway of her doghouse, looking toward me with longing and expectation.

I admit I'm no dog trainer, and it's obvious I had sent my dog the wrong message. That she sat in her doghouse wasn't at all important to me, but she believed that was the way success worked. Somewhere in her little doggy brain, she thought, *If I go in here, he will give me food.*

I never ordered her into her house other than that one time, and I never again rewarded her with food when she went there, but she continued to perform that action for years, believing it would produce the result she wanted from me.

How many people act the same way in regard to success? How many people believe...

If I go into the doghouse...	**then I will get fed.**
If I get a college degree...	then I will have a job.
If I am faithful to my job...	then that job will always be there for me.
If I stay with someone long enough...	then he or she will eventually marry me.
If I get married...	then I will live happily ever after.
If I vote for the right candidate...	then my financial problems will be solved.
If I ignore the problem...	then it will go away.
If I am a good person...	then God will bless me financially and relationally.
If I play the lottery...	then I will get rich.
If I compromise my moral values in a romantic situation...	then I will be loved.
If I pay Social Security...	then I will be taken care of in old age.

If I wait patiently…	then my prince or princess will come.
If I keep my head down and don't make any trouble…	then I will be safe.

People who have this concept of success are always surprised when it doesn't work the way they thought it should. They cry "Unfair!" and feel that life, God, or the universe has cheated them. They did what they were supposed to do, but then life turned around and slapped them when they weren't looking. A woman gets her degree but is unable to get a job in her field. A man goes to church and gives generously, yet he is still impoverished. Another man who paid Social Security all his life has to get a job greeting people at the department-store entrance.

The truly amazing thing about this cataclysmic failure of a belief system is that people rarely conclude their belief system is faulty. Most of the time they will either ignore or forget the results and forge ahead with another doomed endeavor.

The wise, however, recognize patterns of failure and are careful not to repeat them.

What Success Isn't

Several years ago, I sat at a table surrounded by teens and young adults as we all stuffed envelopes for one of my direct-mail campaigns. Nobody seemed to be interacting much, so I thought I'd get the ball rolling.

"So, what do you guys want to do when you get out of school?" I asked.

A girl at the end of the table piped up immediately, "I want to be famous!" she said enthusiastically as heads nodded around the table in agreement.

"Really?" I replied. "But being famous isn't really a vocation, is it? What do you think you would like to be famous for?"

"Oh, I don't care," she answered. "Singing, acting, whatever. I just want to be famous. I think it'd be cool!"

I can't tell you the number of similar conversations I've had with young people all over the country that reflect that same sentiment. But hardly anyone ever looks at the end result and asks himself if, in the unlikely event that he were able to accomplish this dubious goal, he would actually be happy.

Hardly a day goes by without some entertainment show reporting the misdeed of some celebrity. It's always the same story. Only the faces and names change. An actor, a singer, or an athlete becomes rich and famous, and then his life deteriorates into a disastrous mess that becomes fodder for a late-night comedy show. Even some of those who don't destroy themselves with drugs, relationships, and abuse don't seem that happy. So why use the lives of the rich and famous as a template for our own success?

Looking at these people, we have to ask, is that really the best description we have for success? In other words, is that really what we're all shooting for? Is being rich going to be enough? Is being famous all that it's cracked up to be? It certainly doesn't seem so to me.

What Success Is

I believe success can best be defined as the process of fulfilling one's potential. It's really the only definition for success that makes any sense. All of us come into the world with different external and internal gifts, so the only fair way to evaluate our success is to measure our growth.

By external gifts, I mean things that have to do with our circumstances, such as money, location, social status, and the like. By internal gifts, I mean the things that have to do with our person, such as intelligence, athletic ability, attractiveness, and so on.

Let's say a fellow you know named Hal has a net worth of $5 million. Hal is already retired in his early thirties, seems to have plenty of friends, travels around the world, and is known and welcomed everywhere he goes. Would you think of him as successful?

Well, if we define success as the process of fulfilling one's potential, we really need to take a better look at Hal's history and then speculate as to his likely trajectory before we can properly answer that question, don't we?

So let's suppose Hal was born with a silver spoon in his mouth. Just after he turned 21, his father passed away, and Hal inherited $25 million. Hal sees this windfall as his opportunity to have fun, to finally live a life unfettered from responsibility and rigid expectation, so he throws lavish parties and indulges in a hedonistic lifestyle. He hangs out with movie stars and rock stars and is always seen and photographed with the rich, famous, and notorious. Hal enjoys his reputation as a bad boy, and his famous derelict friends let Hal finance all the fun.

Hal has also financed several of his friends' elaborate business schemes, but none of them ever seem to pan out. As Hal's money gradually disappears, so do his famous friends, so Hal redefines and relocates his circle of influence to a more local group of admirers. He now hangs out in your area, where everyone thinks he's a big shot.

That kind of lifestyle is never kind to one's looks or health, so Hal is constantly dealing with a number of health issues that he really doesn't like to discuss. He'd rather fill your ears with tales of days gone by. Hal is great to have around because he tells a great story, but no one thinks of him as a leader or a true friend. He's weathered a few divorces and fathered a child or three here or there, but the exes despise him, and his kids don't know him and don't care to.

Do you still think Hal is successful? Not if you define success as the process of fulfilling one's potential. Unless Hal begins implementing some serious changes that produce growth in his life, Hal's story isn't likely to wind up very happily. The money will continue to deteriorate, and Hal will probably wind up broke and alone.

But what if we painted Hal's history with a different brush? Suppose the Hal you know has about the same net worth, but instead of being born wealthy, Hal came from a single-parent home. Raised by an abusive, alcoholic mother, Hal managed not only to survive childhood but also to put himself through school and start his own business.

Hal recognized the ever-present negative influence of his childhood, so he actively sought personal-growth opportunities, such as counseling, education, and training. He married and had children of his own and has worked hard to not repeat the errors of his upbringing.

Hal constantly gives to his community through volunteerism and contributions and is known by many as a generous and kind soul. He is a friend and lover to his wife and a loving and involved father to his children.

So now you have two pictures of two very different Hals. Which Hal would you define as successful? Almost everyone I know would obviously choose the second scenario. It's growth versus decay. Movement versus inertia. Life versus death.

I am asking you to reexamine and then redefine your picture of success. Instead of asking yourself, *Am I successful?* ask yourself,

> *Am I attempting to fulfill my potential?*
>
> *Am I growing financially, spiritually, and relationally?*
>
> *How have I challenged myself in the past year?*
>
> *Have I progressed in my knowledge and abilities recently?*
>
> *Am I on the road toward accomplishing what I am capable of with my life?*
>
> *Have I been faithful to use and improve the gifts I have been given?*

Fulfilling Your Potential

My first job after I graduated from high school was working in the snack bar at Forrest General Hospital. My responsibilities primarily consisted of pouring fountain drinks and selling candy. For eight hours each day I stood in a hot little room, barely larger than a closet, and fetched candy, cigarettes (back when they still sold cigarettes in hospitals), and fountain drinks for hospital employees. I hated just about every minute of it.

I am amazed that I managed to work that job for almost five years.

During that period of my life, my friends or family occasionally told me that I had a lot of potential. I was always very flattered when I heard this and took this as a huge compliment. I understood it to mean that they saw great intelligence, talent, and latent ability in me. They felt that I was going places and that one day I would be a big deal.

But as I've thought about this statement over the years, I have come to believe it is anything but a compliment. It was no doubt intended as one, but the implication is that the person with potential is not presently living up to it. It might be possible for him to one day do so, but he is not presently.

To comment that an idea or project has potential is quite different. An idea isn't a person. It has no inherent responsibility to bloom, grow, or expand. When an idea doesn't come to fruition, it might be a loss or a setback, but in most cases it isn't a tragedy.

For a person to never strive to reach his potential, for him to remain at the same state of inactivity or dormancy throughout his entire life—in my opinion, that is the very definition of a tragedy. Something sacred has been lost. A life has been wasted. I can't imagine anything sadder than getting to the end of one's life and having done nothing with it.

And you can't identify mediocre people by their job title or dress code. Some people who work in menial jobs, such as my job at the snack bar, are nonetheless in motion. They are growing and reaching for their potential, striving to better themselves and their circumstances. Other people work in nice offices but stagnate day after day, perfectly happy with status quo, drawing a paycheck in return for the absolute minimum effort and output. Which person would you say epitomizes mediocrity?

So how do you go about fulfilling your potential? Where do you begin on the journey toward purpose and meaning? I believe the only way to accomplish this is to harness, develop, and apply your Seven Powers of Success.

The Seven Powers: Your Success Vehicle

In my presentations, I often describe the Seven Powers as something everyone can understand, such as a car. If success is a journey, you're going to need a vehicle to get you on your way.

The Power of Choice is the steering wheel of your success vehicle. You are exactly where you have chosen to be in life. With the decisions you have made, you have either steered your life toward fulfilling your potential or away from it. Each decision you've made has led you to your present position in every area of life—your relationships, your income, your vocation, where you live, how you live, your income, your spirituality…and did I mention your income? The steering wheel is in your hands. Your cognizance and ownership of the Power of Choice has everything to do with where you are right now and where you will be the rest of your life.

The Power of Vision is the windshield of your success vehicle. All the possibilities of your future are viewed through this lens. No one driving toward success should expect to arrive at his destination if his vision is muddied, smeared, or uncertain. Your vision determines your direction, and your direction determines your destination. Those who dismiss the importance of a clear windshield are destined for a rough journey. Making sure that you take the time to examine and develop the Power of Vision so that you can clearly see the possibilities of your future is of paramount importance.

The Power of Mind is the onboard navigational system or GPS of your success vehicle. Paying attention to the development and proper programming of your mind is a critical element in your success journey. Doing so will empower you to successfully navigate your path and avoid the obstacles that lay ahead of you. The odd thing is that so few people pay heed to the development of their mind—specifically, the way their mind processes information. Learning to access, feed, and apply the Power of Mind is the difference between being able to steer around trouble in life and bumping into every obstacle on the way to your destination.

The Power of Action is the accelerator of your success vehicle. Every car is useless unless you engage the ignition system, put the car in gear, and press the accelerator. You may be operating well in the other six of the Seven Powers, but unless you press the accelerator, your success vehicle is going to stay parked in the garage and never take you anywhere. The Power of Action makes the difference between doing and talking, success and mediocrity, fulfillment and frustration, growth and stagnation.

The Power of Failure is the emergency roadside repair kit of your success vehicle. Almost anyone you ask will tell you that the opposite of success is failure, but as I have studied success in my life and in the lives of those people I most admire, I have found the opposite to be true. Failure is a necessary component of success. If success is defined as fulfilling your potential, then in order to do so you will have to try to do things you've never done before. As a natural consequence of doing things you've never done, you will fail sometimes. But if you learn the lessons of that failure and apply them to future endeavors—which will result in your growth—then it stands to reason that failure must be an essential ingredient in your success. No one likes to fail, but realizing the purpose of failure in your life will help you adopt a healthy attitude and approach toward failure. As a result, you will fear it less and embrace the growth opportunities it holds.

The Power of Character is the frame of your success vehicle. Everything of value to you—your finances, your relationships, your reputation, everything you love—rides on the framework of your character. Strong character will carry you over tough terrain and empower you to weather the storms on your journey. A weak, corroded character will leave you broken down, stranded on the road to your dreams. No one has perfect character, but you can still assign value to this area and establish yourself as a person of value in your community, thus safeguarding all that is important to you.

The Power of Belief is the engine of your success vehicle. All vehicles must be driven by a power source, and your Power of Belief energizes all of the rest of your Seven Powers. What you believe, whom you believe in, and where you invest your belief are as critical to your success as an engine is to any car. In order to persevere through difficult times, to move forward when all seems lost, to persist when no one else shares your passion or dreams, you must harness the Power of Belief and make it an active part of your journey.

The Nature of the Beast

Before we start talking about the Seven Powers and how to apply them, I want to consider a couple of important characteristics of the Seven Powers so that you will be able to make the best use of the principles as we cover them.

No One Power Brings Success by Itself

It happened every year without fail on the television show *American Idol*. Early on in each season, a few contestants would have the opportunity of trying out for the three judges. They would confidently walk in, take their place on the small stage, exchange a few words with one or two of the judges, and then belt out the most horrendous version of a pop song imaginable.

The judges would usually try not to laugh during the performance, but after a long day hearing countless contestants, fatigue would set in, and sometimes the laughter would leak out. Afterward, during the evaluation, one of the judges had to inform the contestants that singing was not his or her forte.

Most often, after hearing the bad news, the disappointed contestant would walk out of the studio and go on his way. But sometimes the contestant would stare at the judges uncomprehendingly. Or he would belligerently argue with them, telling them that they must be mistaken, that he was the very epitome of exceptional singing. If the contestant's tirade continued too long or too loud, he would be escorted out of the studio and onto the street.

Watching this spectacle, you can't help but feel sorry for the person being thrown out of the building. He seemed to truly believe that he was destined for greatness, that he had the talent to be a national superstar. There is little question that he fervently, adamantly, passionately believed in himself. But what he failed to understand is that none of the Seven Powers works by itself. You must have a combination of most or all of the Seven Powers of Success working for you if you are to have real success.

It doesn't matter if a person fully and completely believes in himself. If he hasn't used the Power of Choice to choose to get vocal coaching or applied the Power of Action to work hard at the craft of singing, no one is going to take him seriously. The Power of Belief by itself is simply not enough to take you anywhere in life.

The Seven Powers Must Be Used Simultaneously

So using only one of the Seven Powers will not create success in your life. Now I want you to understand that using one power at a time is equally useless. The Seven Powers intermingle and are not independent of each other. The use of one very much affects the others.

The human body is an excellent example of interdependent harmony. All of your organs need all the others to work at the same time if they are to function correctly. Your heart needs oxygen from your lungs. Your lungs need blood from your heart. Your brain needs blood and oxygen to function. All of your body needs nutrients from your digestive system.

The key is that all of these parts need to be functioning *at the same time*.

You can't expect the Power of Choice to do you any good if you aren't actively employing the Power of Action. The Power of Action will be useless if you aren't exercising your Power of Vision, knowing where you want to go and why you are going there. The Seven Powers are interlinked, interactive, and interdependent.

1

The Power of
CHOICE

//

One of my favorite movie scenes of all time is in *The Matrix*. Neo (Keanu Reeves) and Morpheus (Laurence Fishburne) sit facing each other in old leather armchairs. The room they are in mirrors the chairs perfectly. The décor appears to have once been upscale, but now old paper peels off the walls and every surface is coated with a thick layer of dust.

After briefly discussing the concepts of fate and choice, Morpheus tells Neo why it is that Neo has come to this meeting. Like a carnival mind reader, Morpheus looks into Neo's eyes and tells him that he (Neo) senses something is wrong with the world, that even though he can't identify or explain it, he realizes something is amiss.

Morpheus asks Neo if he knows what he is talking about, and Neo correctly guesses he is referring to the Matrix. Morpheus then asks Neo if he would like to know what the Matrix is, and Neo nods his head.

Morpheus tells Neo that he, like everyone around him, is a slave, imprisoned within an invisible jail. He then produces a silver case that holds two pills—one red, the other blue. Each pill represents a choice that Neo has before him. He can either take the red pill and remain imprisoned in his comfortable, familiar, ordinary world, or he can take the blue pill and find out "how deep the rabbit hole goes."

This scene resonates with me because it is a perfect metaphor for the human condition. We are all born into a set of circumstances that includes our looks, our social status, our financial condition, our faith, where we live, how we live…every component is a part of the matrix into which we are born. We unquestioningly accept these circumstances as truth and act accordingly.

Let me put it another way. When we are born, it's as if we walk into a room with a television show called *My Life* playing on the TV. Most people just plop themselves down on the couch and watch that show for the rest of their lives because they don't realize two things: Other channels are available, and they are holding the remote.

It never dawns on most people that we can break out of this matrix and choose a different reality. What would our lives be like if we could swallow a pill or click a button, accept a different truth, and walk a different path? Where would you be? What would your life be like? How would you spend your time?

The first step to choosing your own reality is realizing your Power of Choice.

The Steering Wheel of Your Success Vehicle

Do you remember the story of Adam and Eve? It involved a garden, a snake, and a very relaxed dress code. Sound familiar? The short story is that when Adam and Eve were hanging out in the Garden of Eden, they decided to eat some fruit they weren't supposed to eat and got evicted as a result. It seems landlord and tenant disagreements existed even in biblical times.

I kid about it, but I can't tell you the amount of time theologians and philosophers have spent debating this subject. Was the story a metaphor, or did it really happen? Was the tree a real tree and the fruit real fruit? Was Adam's fig leaf Ralph Lauren or Christian Dior?

Countless books have been written about these things over the ages. But to me, the main point of the story seems to be that choice is a God-given, integral part of our humanity. It is what separates us from the rest of creation and defines us as humans. It is a sacred, special characteristic that we should cherish and value as one of our most precious attributes.

Everything in your life begins and ends with choice—all your success, all your dreams, all your hopes of what your life could be, all your disappointments of what your life has been, where you live, how much money you make, your friends, your lifestyle, your habits…all are deeply rooted in the Power of Choice. Even your beliefs, your perspective, and your principles are products of the choices you make.

Forget what you have learned about genetics determining your destiny. Forget about the ideology that biology determines the outcome of your story. Dismiss the notion that the sum of your being—all that you are capable of and have the possibility of becoming—is already written in the confines of your genetic structure.

Forget about where you were born, who you are related to, or what your family history is. Set aside anything anyone has told you about your future being predetermined by your looks or your innate talent. Ignore the voices that have told you that all life is determined by fate or chance.

Instead, suppose for just a moment that it doesn't matter what you've received from your genetics, your parents, nature, the government, or society. Imagine that the only issue on the table, the only thing that matters in relation to where you go in life, is what you choose to do with what you've been given. It is only after you have considered this possibility that you are beginning to become aware of just how potent the Power of Choice is in your life.

Why Should I Choose?

Early in my speaking career, my main marketing method was telemarketing. Back in those days, I sat at my desk for hours each day making call after call to drum up business. If you wanted to get someone's attention in the days before the Internet, you had to pick up the phone or write a letter.

So day in and day out, I called businesses, churches, and nonprofit organizations and asked to speak to the person in charge. After I got him or her on the line, I began pitching the idea of hosting me for an event or gathering.

Over the years, I made thousands of these calls and, by doing so, got an education that money can't buy. The lessons I learned and the discipline I built making all those calls are invaluable to me now.

Out of all of those phone calls, one sticks out in my memory as especially relevant to the Power of Choice. I was talking on the phone with a friend who was an Ohio businessman, telling him about a particular employee of mine. I complained that she never seemed to follow my direction and that I was constantly having to bring her back on course. When left on her own, she would do almost anything other than what I had instructed her to do.

My friend patiently listened to my whining and then chuckled and said, "Well, Charles, if you don't run your business, someone else will."

I've since realized the truth of those words and learned that they apply not only to business but every area of one's life. If you are not consciously making decisions about your marriage, career, finances, family, living arrangements, or health, you can bet someone else is making those decisions for you or shortly will be.

Not Making a Decision Is Making a Decision

Shortly after I moved to Atlanta in 1985, I took a job in a men's clothing store at Gwinnett Place Mall while I got my bearings in a new city. A few months afterward, I fell for a brown-eyed brunette named Laura who worked in the gift shop right across from the store where I worked.

Our relationship was pretty rocky at first. She was a 20-year-old college coed, barely out of high school, and I was a 25-year-old who came charging at her out of nowhere, wanting a serious relationship. I fell for her almost immediately, but her feelings for me were...inconsistent at best. She definitely liked being pursued but was indecisive about her feelings for me. She wasn't sure if she was ready to commit to a long-term relationship or if I was the right guy for her. The messages I got from her were mixed—she loved me, she loved me not. This yo-yo dynamic went on for quite some time until she broke off the relationship completely. After a couple of months of being apart, we started dating each other again, but the yo-yo soon reappeared. She just couldn't seem to make up her mind whether she really loved me.

This back-and-forth emotional roller coaster was torturous for me. I really cared for this young lady and did my best to win her heart, but nothing ever seemed to close the deal. Finally, I made the decision that things could not go on the way they had been going. I told her that if she didn't make up her mind, I was gone. I set a date (which I kept to myself) and decided that if she was still playing games by then, I would walk away. I felt that I didn't have forever to wait for someone to make up her mind about me and that I deserved someone who wasn't constantly questioning her love for me.

Laura tells me now that she could tell I meant business, so she concluded it was time to quit playing games and commit to the relationship. We were engaged not long afterward and have been married since then.

Through the whole ordeal, Laura and I both learned an important principle: Not making a decision is making a decision.

Some people would like to believe that putting off a decision indefinitely is an option. It is not. Life isn't a pond. It isn't static. It's a river that keeps flowing. People don't wait around forever for your decision. Time doesn't stand still while you make up your mind. The earth keeps spinning, seasons keep changing, money keeps changing hands, people keep living and dying. At some point, the ship sails and the decision is made.

- By neglecting to plan for your future, you are ensuring that you will be a burden to someone else in your latter years.

- To let someone drive drunk is to decide to endanger his life and the life of every person he meets on the road.

- By not standing up for your rights, you are choosing to let people take advantage of you.

- When you do not educate or equip yourself to produce an income, you are choosing a life of financial struggle and poverty.

- If you choose not to forgive, you choose to let the offending party own a piece of you.

- By not deciding to transition out of a job you hate, you are deciding to live an unproductive life of voluntary servitude.

- By not saying or doing anything when you see someone committing an illegal or immoral act, you are choosing to aid the wrongdoer.

- When one parent is abusive and the other doesn't intervene, the passive parent becomes a partner in the abuse.

- When you turn on the television without having a specific program you want to watch, or continue to watch a program after you know it holds no interest for you, you are deciding to forfeit your free time and let a television executive choose what you watch.

- The man who can't decide between two jobs will inevitably lose both positions if he doesn't commit to one of them.

- If you neglect to eat healthy foods and get sufficient exercise, you are choosing a life of health challenges.

You Owe It to Me

A number of years ago I sat in a Shoney's restaurant with Joey and Herb discussing the challenges of running a nonprofit organization. Both Joey and I had started charitable organizations, but neither of us was very successful at getting contributors. The mood at the table was sour at best. I sensed that Joey was almost angry that nobody seemed to understand the value of all the good things he was trying to do in his community. "Why don't people jump in with both feet and give a little?" Joey asked.

I nodded my head in agreement. My experience and sentiment mirrored Joey's pretty closely. It seemed to me that he had a valid point.

He continued, "I mean, if someone would just pay for my postage or gas every month, it would help!"

I contributed my own tales of woe to the conversation, but they didn't really add any illumination or insight to the subject. Joey and I were just as perplexed after our discussion as we were when we began it.

I hadn't really noticed that Herb wasn't joining in the gripe session. Joey and I were too busy paddling down the river of self-pity and enjoying the ride. Herb listened patiently for a good while and let Joey and me get it all out of our systems. Finally, Herb smiled and shook his head.

"Listen, you guys," Herb said. "You seem to think the world owes you something just because you showed up. You think everyone ought to get behind you because you're so wonderful and are doing such wonderful things."

I looked at Joey, Joey looked at me, and we both looked at Herb. It seemed to me that Herb had it about right.

"Yeah, so, what's your point?" Joey asked, smiling.

"My point is this," Herb said, exasperated. "Instead of sitting around wishing someone would come along and give you money so you can do some good in the world, why don't you figure out a way to make some money so you can not only do something positive but also be the answer to someone else's prayer and help him finance his project?"

It would take me years to fully digest those words. Herb was implying that Joey and I had an entitlement mentality. The source of our frustration was that we expected someone to help us, and were disappointed when it didn't happen.

An entitlement mentality is the belief that someone—a family member, a friend, your employer, the government, or God—owes you something. The individual who adheres to this life mind-set usually thinks he is due because he…

> is a good person
>
> is a special person
>
> has suffered
>
> believes himself incapable or insufficient
>
> has fantasized about a better lifestyle

You're Entitled to Know the Truth About Entitlement

We usually think or hear about entitlement in regard to government spending, but entitlement thinking is so much more pervasive than in just that one area. It is everywhere and in every part of our lives. Often we have an entitlement mentality without even knowing it. If you are an entitlement thinker, you might find yourself thinking or saying any one of these statements:

- Everybody has the right to be happy.
- Things cost too much. Prices should be lower.
- My parents should continue to take care of me when I'm an adult.
- My children should take care of me in my old age because I took care of them when they were little.
- My employer should pay for my health benefits.
- It's God's job to take care of me.
- If I am a person of faith, I will have a lot of money.
- I should have been married by this time in my life.
- I expect to be in a relationship with a supermodel (without being a supermodel myself).
- The government should create more jobs.
- The government should take care of my food, shelter, health, transportation, education, protection, and retirement.
- All citizens are owed a living wage regardless of their job.
- I went to college, so I should be able to get the kind of job I want and make the kind of money I want.
- My child's teacher needs to accept my child's behavior and adapt her behavior toward my child accordingly.
- All teachers should be paid more.

I understand that a few of the items on the list might give you pause. Shouldn't we care for other people? Shouldn't we have a safety net in our society for those who have fallen on hard times?

Absolutely! But understand that there is a huge difference between feeling an obligation to care for another's needs and demanding that someone else cares for yours. It's the difference between wanting to give a gift to someone and demanding that you receive one yourself.

One of the worst things about entitlement thinking is that it robs you of the ownership of your decisions. If you are waiting for someone to give you something, you are placing the Power of Choice in his hands and not your own. In essence, you are saying that you do not decide for yourself what your future holds, that your fortune is in the hands of someone else, that someone else will decide whether you receive money, care, love, and health. You are limiting your potential to that which someone else can or will provide.

One of the most precious assets given to mankind is our Power of Choice, and we should never surrender that power easily. Entitlement and choice are two conflicting principles that cannot be practiced simultaneously. Either you place your trust and hope in someone doing something for you, or you choose to create your own solutions.

It's Not My Fault

Another reason people don't exert their Power of Choice is a little five-letter word called blame.

When I grew up, there were three choices for television viewing: ABC, NBC, and CBS. If you didn't like the programs on any of those channels...you were out of luck. Fortunately, some great programs aired back then, such as *The Brady Bunch*, *The Partridge Family*, *Sanford and Son*, and *The Bob Newhart Show*. Most of these shows continue to enjoy popularity even today.

One very popular show in the early 1970s featured the comedy of a young man named Clerow Wilson Jr., better known as Flip Wilson. It's hard to communicate to people today just how enormously popular Flip Wilson was in the early '70s. In just a few short years, Flip established himself as not just the top African-American comedian in the country, but the most popular comedian period, regardless of race. For four years Flip was the undisputed king of comedy.

One of his main strengths as a performer was his ability to create original, lovable characters. Long before Martin Lawrence dressed up as Big Momma, way before Tyler Perry donned a wig and skirt to become Madea, Flip was dressing up as the confident, sassy, strong Geraldine Jones. I remember my entire family doubling over with laughter in our living room as we watched Flip sashaying across the stage as Geraldine.

Flip's character, Geraldine, would often spout, "The devil made me do it!" as a paper-thin attempt to explain her questionable behavior.

I think that line became a national catchphrase because Flip delivered it so well and because everyone could relate to a character playing the blame game. It is human nature to want to blame someone or something when we fall short or when we haven't accomplished what we or others feel we should or might have.

Blame rarely wears its own face, but instead disguises itself as either a plausible or unlikely explanation. (The devil made me do it!) See if any of these blame statements sound familiar to you.

> Everybody else was doing it.
>
> I'm not responsible for that decision.
>
> It just wasn't God's plan (or timing or will).
>
> It's not up to me.
>
> I could never lose that much weight.
>
> That's above my pay grade.
>
> It wasn't in the cards for me. It wasn't my destiny.
>
> The relationship didn't work out because he was such a jerk.
>
> I didn't have the money to attend college.
>
> I didn't come from the right neighborhood or know the right people.
>
> I'm not the type to kiss up to the bigwigs.
>
> The economy has been down, so business has been a little slow.

I gave it a shot, but it didn't work out.

If you were in my shoes, you wouldn't have done any better.

Some people might think such statements don't represent blame, but are simply explanations of why things haven't worked out. What could be so bad about allowing yourself a bit of philosophical elbow room in dealing with life's disappointments?

Maybe you noticed that a couple of these statements adopt a posture of spirituality. What's so bad about that? Wouldn't such comments reflect a faith in God? Isn't it laudable to proclaim to the world that when things go in a different direction from what you have hoped or planned, they are still part of God's divine plan?

Blame is in the habit of wearing attractive disguises. When you pull the mask off such statements as the ones above and take a look at what is really being said, you will always find the same old ugly blame. Let's look at a few examples.

It just wasn't God's plan (or timing or will). (I have no responsibility for the outcome of this situation because I am taking the philosophical stand that God usurped the outcome for his own purposes.)

That's above my pay grade. (I don't have to come up with an answer or solution because I am not paid to do so. Someone else in my organization might have the answers, but I'm not required to.)

The economy's been down, so business has been a little slow. (The economy is not vigorous, so it is acceptable that my business is producing less money.)

I gave it a shot, but it didn't work out. (All that is required of me is to make some sort of attempt. I am not responsible for a positive result as long as I tried.)

Do those translations sound coldhearted? I don't mean for them to. I think of them as rather liberating. To allow yourself to blame is to allow yourself to lose. I don't want to go through life like that, believing that other people, situations, God, my job, or whatever can arbitrarily yank the rug out from underneath me. I would rather not submit to the tyranny of blame.

The Blame Trade

And what's so bad about blame?

Only this: If you allow yourself to blame, you are giving up your Power of Choice. When you blame, you are saying you had no choice, no options, no control in the situation and therefore aren't responsible for the outcome. You allow yourself an out. You are assigning some entity, organization, or event all of the responsibility for your outcome of your situation.

The danger of such thinking is that when you give up responsibility for a part of your life, you surrender possession of it. To give up your ownership of something is to give up your power to choose. A person who doesn't own an object doesn't have the legal or moral right to choose what happens to it.

So the part that feels so good about blame—the reassignment of responsibility—has a hidden dark side. By indulging in blame, you surrender your power to choose a solution. Blame saves you from the emotional weight of fully owning your failure, but it also prevents you from fulfilling your goals, hopes, expectations, and dreams.

Choosing Not to Blame

People who are used to employing the Power of Choice don't allow themselves to blame. It doesn't matter to them that the economy is down. They will choose to do something to improve their business. It doesn't matter if the world is full of jerks. They will find their way around those folks and surround themselves with a better grade of people. It doesn't matter if they didn't have enough money for college. They will explore other ways to pay for their education or succeed without a formal education.

HERE'S A THOUGHT...

What if your life is a gift from God and what you do with it is your responsibility, not God's?

People who exploit the Power of Choice know that blame is a cop-out and gets you nowhere. For every scenario that has been blamed for failure, countless people have managed to overcome it and achieve success.

Lock Me Up but Make Sure I'm Well Fed

A number of years ago, I had a conversation with a friend named Neal about government and the part it should play in the lives of its citizens. Neal felt that a government should take care of everyone living in that particular country. I asked him how far that philosophy extended. Did that mean government should take care of our food, shelter, clothing, health care, and transportation? Where exactly did Neal feel we should draw the line with this caretaking?

Neal thought about that for a minute and then replied, "Well, I guess the government should take care of all of those things."

"Seriously?" I responded. "To provide those things, wouldn't the government (meaning people other than you) be responsible for making all the major decisions about your life, including where you work, what you do for a living, where you live, who your doctor is, what you drive (if you drive at all), and what kind of food you eat? Would that be okay with you?"

Neal, whom I should mention was a hardworking entrepreneur in the printing business, listened to my question and then surprised me with one of the most offensive answers I could have imagined. "Yeah, that would be all right. As long as the government was taking care of all my needs, I wouldn't mind those decisions being made for me."

"You can't be serious," I said. "What you're describing is the very definition of slavery. That's SLAVE-ER-Y! You're saying that you would give up the right to almost every important decision in your life just so that you can be fed and housed and have your basic material needs met. How can you even begin to think that's a good idea? Isn't that a slap in the face of every person who has been enslaved, of every color and nationality throughout history?"

Neal laughed at my response and said, "Well, it wouldn't really be slavery. Nobody would own me. It would be the government taking care of me."

I am just as stunned thinking about that mentality now as I was when I heard it 20 years ago. Why would anyone willingly stick out both hands, saying, "Chain me up and make me your slave. Oh, but make sure that the AC is turned on and that I have a Big Mac"?

I cannot comprehend anyone making that decision, but I do understand the thinking behind it. Some people don't want a choice. They want other people to decide for them. They would rather not be responsible for their own lives. They would rather have someone else take care of them.

It's Elementary

I was in my early thirties by the time I discovered Sir Arthur Conan Doyle's wonderful books about master sleuth Sherlock Holmes. Like everyone else, I had been exposed to the character of Holmes all my life, but I had somehow missed reading any of his adventures. Once I read one book, though, I was hooked and eagerly devoured each tale, one right after the other, until I had consumed every story.

The thing I loved so much about Holmes was his ability to use his powers of observation and deductive reasoning to extract meaning from the most ordinary things. In the stories, Holmes often only has to look at a few fragments of evidence before producing the name of the perpetrator or, at very least, the next essential step in solving the crime.

I believe all of us have a bit of that same ability to observe and deduce. No, not to the degree that Holmes exhibited, but certainly enough to accomplish a little exercise I want you to do.

If you were sitting in front of Sherlock Holmes right now and he were to examine your life for the past five years, what would he deduce in regard to your Power of Choice?

If he were to look at your relationships—the way you normally interact with your family, friends, and coworkers—would he say you were choosing health, growth, and intimacy? Or would he deduce from your lack of healthy communication that those relationships were stagnant and stale? What would the evidence lead him to think?

If he were to look at your education—applying yourself to the goal of learning by reading informative materials—would there be enough evidence to convince him that you are employing the Power of Choice? Would your daily actions and behavior convince him that you have chosen to continue to educate yourself about not only your profession but also about your health, your world, your relationships?

Or would the evidence convince him that you haven't chosen to educate yourself at all?

If he were to examine your professional life—the way you behave in regard to your job, your career, your organization—would he come to the conclusion that you have chosen to move forward, to do whatever you could to enhance your growth opportunities, to be of value to those around you and your organization? Or would he be forced to conclude that you are just treading water? That you're showing up, doing your time, and then punching out?

If he were to look at your spirituality—your recognition that you are not only flesh and bone but also an eternal spirit—would it be obvious to him that you are addressing the growth, nourishment, and well-being of your soul? Would your daily activities prove that you are cognizant of the importance of addressing the deeper needs of your being?

If he were to look at your physical life—how you treat your body, what you eat, and how often you exercise—would he deduce that you choose to value your health? That you make decisions that will affect the well-being of your body? Would he see that you are aware that your health is your choice?

Stepping outside of your life for a moment can help you honestly evaluate how you are applying the Power of Choice. I want you to see that your life, your path, your destination, is truly in your hands.

If your life isn't what you want it to be or isn't headed in that direction, you have sacrificed and yielded the Power of Choice in some area. This is not intended to be a statement of condemnation but rather of empowerment. Once you are aware of a weakness, you can begin to correct it.

> **HERE'S A THOUGHT...**
>
> People who employ the Power of Choice make decisions. People who don't, make excuses.

Let's Go Shopping

Every minute I spend shopping in a department store or grocery store is usually excruciatingly painful. But somehow, whenever I enter any Home Depot, or Lowe's, an amazing thing happens. All that loathing for shopping magically disappears! I can wander around in those stores for hours and not even notice any time has passed at all.

I discovered this in 2004 when I bought a home that had been in foreclosure and decided to remodel it myself. I had never done any remodeling at all, so every day was a learning experience, and most days required a trip to the hardware store.

I would drive to the renovation house, work a little bit, and then discover I needed about five essential remodeling tools. I'd hop in my car and run up to the hardware store and then aimlessly wander around for hours at a time, exploring anything and everything on the shelves. After wasting an untold amount of time doing this, I decided my problem was that I had too many choices in front of me. When I am looking at a wall of products and they all look the same, it's difficult to know where to start, so my tendency is to do nothing but stand there and look at the wall. Sometimes having too many options can be paralyzing.

I decided that if I were to make any progress on the renovation, I needed to focus on my specific task by knowing exactly what I needed before I walked into the store.

Tools for Exercising Your Power of Choice

The danger at this point of conveying the Power of Choice principles and encouraging you to start employing this power in your life is that the areas of choice are virtually limitless. I don't want to send you into the Power of Choice store only to have you wander around forever, looking at all the possibilities but never making a purchase.

So I'd like to put on my orange or blue apron and lead you around the store so you can become familiar with some of the areas of choice that you have available. The aisles I'm suggesting are the ones that I think are the most interesting and important. They contain some of the tools that I have found most helpful and liberating on my success journey.

Choose Who You Are

One of my heroes—a man who embodies all of the Seven Powers but especially the Power of Choice—is Portland, Oregon, native Bill

Porter. You may have never heard of Bill. He's not a rock star or an actor. He's not a politician or an athlete. In many respects, Bill is just a normal guy. He gets up each day, goes to work, pays his bills, and spends time with friends and family.

But Bill has lived his ordinary life in such an extraordinary manner with such an extraordinary attitude, a wonderful book was written about his life—*Ten Things I Learned from Bill Porter*. The book inspired a movie, *Door to Door*, starring William H. Macy (he won Emmy Awards as actor and cowriter). Both the book and the movie are extremely inspirational, and I highly recommend them.

As I learned about Bill, one of the first things I noticed was his amazing work ethic. He starts each day at 4:45. He doesn't need to get on the bus to go to work until 7:20, but he needs that much time to do two things—get dressed and eat. Bill needs the extra time because he was born with cerebral palsy, a condition that hampers his speech and motor skills. His mind is wholly unaffected by his condition, but he has a difficult time doing tasks that most of us take for granted, such as buttoning his shirt cuffs and tying his shoes. Bill recognizes the importance of looking one's best, so each day he catches the bus to downtown Portland, where he has an arrangement with the bellhops at a downtown hotel to help him with his shoelaces and shirt-sleeve buttons. Bill then boards another bus at 8:30 so he can make it to work by 9:00.

What type of a job would you suppose might be right for Bill? What type of job would you recommend for someone with Bill's talents and abilities?

As soon as Bill graduated from high school, his father strongly urged him to get a job, so Bill began maintaining neighbors' lawns, earning about four dollars a week. He then graduated to his second job, fundraising for United Cerebral Palsy by selling various household items. After that, he created his own gift catalog and sold items door-to-door.

That job worked for Bill for a while, but when his father's health deteriorated and his family's future became a concern, Bill began looking for better employment opportunities.

He began his search by visiting the State of Oregon Employment

Department. Through their efforts he was placed as a pharmacy stock clerk, a Goodwill cashier, a dock worker at Salvation Army, and a phone worker with the Veterans Rehabilitation Center. At each job, Bill gave a valiant effort, but being ill-suited to each occupation, he was let go in short order.

Bill continued to go back to the state employment office day after day to look for additional jobs, but after five months, he was politely told he didn't need to come back anymore. Bill was considered by the state to be unemployable, and they suggested that he stay home and collect disability pay.

Their assessment of Bill and his abilities could not have been more wrong. Bill decided that he wanted to pursue a career in sales as his father had done, so he began looking for sales jobs himself, answering ads in the paper and getting rejected many times.

Finally, Bill answered an ad for a sales position with Watkins Incorporated, a company known for selling household items, such as detergent, spices, and cleaning supplies, door-to-door. During his interview, Bill managed to sell the Watkins representative on the idea of giving him a territory to work on a trial basis.

Bill's new sales territory was in one of the worst neighborhoods imaginable, so he had a couple of problems to solve if he wanted to make his new position permanent. First, crime was high in the neighborhood, so he had to worry not only about selling but also about not getting hurt. Second, many of the residents were impoverished, and Bill was paid only on commissions.

When I'm telling Bill's story in my motivational program, I usually stop at this point and look at my crowd. In my head I can almost hear the theme song of *Rocky III*, "Eye of the Tiger." In the movie, the song depicts the inner drive of a fighter, a hidden courage and aggressiveness that comes from deep within. I survey my audience and wonder if any Bill Porters are out there. Does anyone in my audience (or anyone reading this book for that matter) have the confidence and drive necessary to voluntarily take one of the worst sales territories possible? Would anyone say, "Yes! Give me the worst area you have, in the worst part of town, and I will make it work. I will survive and prosper where others have failed"?

Are there still any people in the world like that? You bet there are. But that's the thing. You can't tell who they're likely to be. Bill was passed over by dozens of companies because he didn't fit their notion of what success is supposed to look like. When I'm looking at an audience, I don't have the ability to see inside people's hearts, to see their inner fight, their "Eye of the Tiger." The mild-mannered, middle-aged man or diminutive older woman might have a fiercely competitive spirit with a rod of steel in his or her spine. So I'm just left to wonder who in my audience would fit that description.

Well, the rest of the story is that Bill faithfully worked his territory and managed to make a living working in that area. After a while Bill transitioned into a better territory and became one of the best salesmen in the company. One of Bill's proudest achievements is that about 40 people who told Bill to go away and not come back are now counted among his more than 500 regular customers. When Bill is asked what his greatest obstacle is, he insists that he has no obstacles. In his mind there are no barriers, no limitations.

I chose Bill's story to represent the Power of Choice because Bill chose not to let other people's picture of him define who he is. Instead of accepting and adopting the opinions of the so-called experts, Bill chose to be something he wanted to be. Instead of receiving a government disability check, Bill chose to be a businessman. Instead of accepting pity for his circumstances, Bill chose a life that encourages others to fulfill their potential and strive to be all they are capable of being. Instead of being defined by the kind of man he's not, he chose to be defined by the extraordinary kind of man he is.

No one I know would have blamed Bill for taking the disability check. No one I know would have judged him for giving up when everyone else around him told him to quit. But Bill isn't that kind of guy. He doesn't see himself as a victim, but as victorious.

Think about the challenges you now face. What is standing in the way of your success? What will you choose to do about the things that seem to block your way? Will you accept a reality that someone else has given to you, or will you choose to be the one who defines who you are?

Choose Your Attitude

The very first thing you have to choose in life is your attitude, your disposition, the way you view the world. Most people allow their circumstances to dictate their attitude, never realizing they have any say in the matter. If the sun is shining, they feel great. If it's raining, they are in a foul mood. If work is going well, they feel good about themselves. If people treat them poorly, they think poorly of themselves. All of us have these tendencies, but truly successful people have trained themselves to resist the temptation of allowing circumstances to form their attitude.

Why is having the right attitude that important? Simply put, your attitude determines your perspective, your perspective determines your direction, and your direction determines your destination. In other words...

- Your attitude determines where you look and what you look at.
- Where you look determines which way you walk.
- The direction you walk has everything to do with where you wind up.

When I was in driver's education class in high school, I remember being told that I should never look into the headlights of oncoming traffic, especially not late at night, when I was tired. I was told to look straight ahead, or better yet, to look at the white line on the right side of the road. Why? Because it is human nature to steer in the direction we are looking. The white line on the side of the road is a constant. It never changes, and focusing on it will ensure that you drive in a straight line. Many a wreck has been caused by someone sleepily staring into the headlights of another vehicle and then veering into oncoming traffic.

Likewise, when you focus on the negative in your life, you will develop the tendency toward negativity. You will find a way to steer yourself into more trouble, more problems, more difficulty. On the other hand, when you are looking at what is working and what you have going for you, you will find yourself steering toward solutions, possibilities, and answers.

I believe one of the reasons Bill Porter has been so successful is that he doesn't perceive obstacles. He certainly recognizes and confronts challenges in his world, but his attitude causes him to see a world of possibilities rather than limitations. Those possibilities have led him to the implementation and execution of a plan that has led to worldwide recognition and admiration.

> **HERE'S A THOUGHT...**
>
> People who use the Power of Choice make tough decisions to successfully negotiate the transitions of life.

Choose Your Community

When Jerry Seinfeld described Kramer, the lovable goofball character from the hit television show *Seinfeld*, he explained that some of the friends we make in life are our friends simply because of their proximity. They live right across the hall from us, they go to church with us, we work with them...so eventually they become our friends.

But what if instead of accidentally choosing our friends, we intentionally chose them? What if we decided what type of people we want or need in our lives and then constructed our social framework around that paradigm?

Ask yourself what type of person you need in your life. Are the people in your interpersonal community givers or takers? What kind of person are you in your community? Are you the type of person whom everyone leans on but who receives no support in return? Or are you the person who expects everyone else to help you but isn't contributing anything to anyone else?

Who are you intentionally or unintentionally choosing for your community? Are you satisfied with your choices? What choices do you need to make in order to build or renovate your support community so that it will be more to your liking?

Choose Your Family Dynamic

A little Mexican restaurant near my house has a great all-you-can-eat Sunday brunch bar. So the other day, right after church, I took my wife and kids over to see how much damage we could do to the owner's bottom line. As we ate our lunch, I noticed the family at the table next to us sat very still, their attention focused toward their laps. The kids were intently focused on their video games, and the parents had disappeared into their texting. They didn't talk to each other or even acknowledge one another's existence the entire time they were in the restaurant.

I couldn't help but wonder if this was how they always interacted—or rather, didn't interact. Did the parents talk with the kids only when the kids needed something from them or needed to be scolded? Why would parents choose this dynamic for their family?

Maybe I misread the situation or just caught that family on an off day, but either way, it made me think. A friend of mine died unexpectedly a couple years ago while he was estranged from his family. There was no warning, no time for final words. This kind of thing happens every day, but do we heed the warning and apply the lesson these stories tell?

The realization that life is short and this is not a dress rehearsal can be an impetus for implementing the Power of Choice. Whatever time we are given must be utilized wisely. That means taking advantage of our time with our family by engaging them, which is a fancy way of saying we need to be talking to each other. We need to interact with each other directly and not allow ourselves to accept adjacent relationships as a standard.

What do you want your family to look like? No, you can't control your children's actions, nor your parents' or husband's or wife's or anyone else's, but you can control your own. What choices do you need to make in order to create the type of family dynamic you want?

Choose to Be Your Best

In Charles Dickens's *A Christmas Carol*, Ebenezer Scrooge is led by the ghost of Christmas future to a cemetery and forced to look at his own gravestone. The inscription had only his name, yet it was a symbol of terror and despair for Scrooge, a physical manifestation of a life misspent.

Suppose for a moment that you and I were to take a similar trip to the future and look down at your gravestone. What do you imagine the epitaph might read? Will we find words that hail you as victorious and reflect your value to your community?

- "Here lies a noble father, faithful friend, and beloved companion."
- "Here lies a woman who tirelessly gave of herself to help those less fortunate so that their suffering might be eased."
- "Here lies one who treated this life as a gift and lived each moment to the fullest."

Or will the words be laced with mediocrity?

- "Here lies the body of Bill Jones. He lived. He died."
- "Here lies the body of Samantha Crawford. We, who were called her friends, didn't know her passions, abilities, or dreams, if indeed she possessed any at all."
- "Here lies Edward Martin, who worked as little as possible, doing the least he could while still drawing a paycheck. He cared for few, liked even fewer, and helped none."

How will your gravestone read? You might say it won't matter to you after you're gone, but fortunately, I am asking while you are still alive. So what would yours say?

Maybe that's too morbid of an exercise for you, so let me ask you in another way. Let's say *Time* magazine has decided to select their Person of the Year from 100 randomly selected individuals. Your name has been chosen, and a public-relations representative has asked you to create a one-sheet summation of your life.

What kind of picture of your life would emerge? Would the PR rep come away with a picture of a vibrant, energized individual who is contributing to his workplace, family, and community in a meaningful and passionate way? Or would the piece read something like a grocery list?

> He goes to work each day, does a little bit, and then clocks out and goes to lunch. He punches back in, works a bit more, and then goes home, where he'll eat supper and then watch television for the rest of the night. The next day he will get up and do the same thing. His work is adequate but uninspired. His relationships are taken for granted, and his health is abused with bad habits and a poor lifestyle.

Nobody I know would want to be described that way. No one wants to be characterized as mediocre. If success is defined as fulfilling one's potential, then you must endeavor to be your best if you are to be successful.

Today, will you choose to just get by doing the least and being the least that you are capable of being, or will you choose to deliver your best to those with whom you live and work?

What Else?

Did I miss any areas in which you can apply the Power of Choice? Absolutely! The choices available to you are limitless. Once you begin to be aware of your Power of Choice, you realize that every part of your life is a product of your decisions. But you should know and understand that having the privilege, the ownership, and the responsibility of choice doesn't mean that every choice you make is correct.

In one of the final scenes in the movie *Indiana Jones and the Last Crusade*, Indiana finds himself in a room full of goblets, one of which is the fabled Holy Grail. An ancient knight who is the guardian of the Holy Grail watches as the villain of the movie hastily grabs one of the goblets and drinks from it, hoping to gain eternal life. Rather than a long life, though, his quick decision results in a rather rapid and grisly death. The ancient knight observes the villain's actions and simply says, "He chose poorly."

Indiana must now choose a goblet. He takes a moment, thinks about his decision carefully, and then drinks from the goblet he selected. He turns around and faces the knight, who states, "You have chosen wisely."

In real life, you don't need a knight to follow you around and make pronouncements regarding the wisdom or folly of your actions. The consequences of your actions will do that for you. The trick, of course, is to choose wisely. Learning the rest of the Seven Powers will help you do just that. I want you to think of the six remaining Powers as choices that you can make. As we continue, I suggest that you choose to...

> Clarify your Power of Vision
>
> Apply your Power of Mind
>
> Engage your Power of Action
>
> Adopt the Power of Failure
>
> Build your Power of Character
>
> Invest in your Power of Belief

POWER OF CHOICE APPLICATION QUESTIONS—
Getting a Grip on Your Steering Wheel

1. Name one area of your life in which you have left control up to someone else.

2. Name one area of your life in which you have used blame to surrender your Power of Choice. ("I'm overweight because of my genes." "My sales are down because of the economy.")

3. Name one time in your life that you have made a decision

by not making a decision. How should you have handled that situation?

4. Name one area of your life that you feel should be someone else's responsibility. Is your answer a reflection of an entitlement mentality?

5. What one choice will you make today that will help you grasp the steering wheel of choice more firmly?

GROUP DISCUSSION QUESTIONS

1. Relate a story of a time when you made the right choice and how that affected your life.

2. In what area(s) of your life have you allowed others to determine your destiny?

2

The Power of
VISION

As I drove away from Holland, Michigan, I knew I might be in real trouble. I had read about blizzards and seen them on TV plenty of times, but I had never experienced one firsthand. Driving east on I-196, I could see the dim outline of dark shapes punctuating the whiteness on either side of my car. I soon realized that these shapes were cars that had driven nose-first into the ditches along the road.

I have to admit I was pretty nervous. Did I say nervous? I meant I was terrified. Driving down the road in a raging blizzard with no visibility really rattled my cage. It was the first weekend in February 2007. I had just completed the first of two events I was doing in the western part of Michigan. I was driving from Holland to Kalamazoo, where I was booked to do a program for several hundred people that night. I didn't want to disappoint them by not showing up, so I decided to drive through the storm. The problem was, I didn't want to die trying to get there either. So I crept along at five or ten miles per hour, gripping the steering wheel in terror.

I'm not exaggerating when I tell you that I couldn't see more than five feet ahead of me. After about an hour, I no longer saw cars in the ditches—or any cars anywhere else on the road for that matter. All I saw was white, white, and more white. Inside the car, it was white-knuckled driving as I drove down the road, praying as hard as I knew how to pray. I was hoping the Lord would send some angels to nudge me back on the road if I started skidding. And for all I know, a whole battalion of them could have been right outside my window, but I would never have known it because all I saw was white. Because you're reading this book, you know that I lived to tell the tale, but unfortunately I didn't have a copy of this book with me at the time, so my fate was up in the air as far as I was concerned.

At one point, I stopped my car in the middle of the interstate, stepped out, and looked around to make sure I was still on the road. It was the only time I've ever stepped out onto the middle of a major interstate. I hope it will be the last. I was terrified of getting out of my car for fear of another vehicle not seeing me and ramming me from behind. But I felt I had to do it. I simply could not see where I was going.

After a couple of hours, the storm thinned as I moved away from Lake Michigan, where the brunt of the storm was focused. I finally could see the road and finished my drive to Kalamazoo, where I did a program that same evening. Unlike people in the South, where I live, people in Michigan apparently come out to events even if it's snowing.

The Windshield of Your Success Vehicle

The Power of Vision is the lens through which you view the possibilities of your journey. If your windshield is obstructed or blurry, you're going to have a hard time telling whether you're on the right path in life—or whether you are still on the road at all.

How many people wander through life in a blizzard of bewilderment, unable to see five feet in front of them? How many people drive off course and never even notice? Or how many people notice that they've hit an obstacle and aren't going anywhere but have no idea it was their lack of vision that landed them where they are?

Most people who wear glasses or contact lenses can tell you exactly what it felt like the first time they viewed the world through their new lenses. I was in fifth grade by the time anyone noticed my vision was impaired. I couldn't see the chalkboard in school, and my grades were suffering. I had headaches at the end of the day from all the squinting I did. I also became more introverted because I couldn't see people's expressions.

After I failed an eye exam at school, Mom and Dad took me to an optometrist-ophthalmologist, who determined that I needed glasses. We ordered the glasses and then went back about a week later to pick them up and get them fitted.

I remember wearing my new glasses home from the doctor's office as if it were yesterday. I was amazed that I could see each blade of grass and every leaf on the trees. From the backseat of the car, I excitedly told my parents about each new wonder I saw with my new glasses. It's an amazing thing to not be able to see, to not even know you can't see, and then suddenly receive the gift of vision.

One of the most important components of this story is that even with all the symptoms of nearsightedness I evinced, I was completely clueless that I had a problem. I had never been nearsighted before, I didn't know what it was, and I certainly didn't have the ability to self-diagnose my condition. Additionally, for quite some time, no one around me knew I had a problem either.

My point is that you don't have to be aware that your vision is bad to suffer the consequences. You can walk through the world, bumping into things, and be completely oblivious that you have a problem.

What Is Vision?

The United States fundamentally changed on June 29, 1956, the day the Interstate Highway System was established by the National Interstate and Defense Highways Act of 1956.

Anyone born in the last 50 years can hardly imagine travel in the United States before the interstate system. You just couldn't get there from here, or to anywhere from anywhere else for that matter. Up until that time, if you wanted to travel, you needed a map and someone to read it as you drove a spiderweb system of two-lane highways through cornfields and one-traffic-light towns.

Then came the interstate system, and travel became easier than ever.

Families all over America hopped in their cars and took off to see the country, visit long-lost relatives, or just follow the road to see where it took them.

A visionary young man named Cecil B. Day took note of this burgeoning trend and concluded that all these travelers would need a place to stop at night. That place would need to be conveniently located next to the interstate and priced so that families could afford to stay there. Mr. Day opened his first hotel in 1970 and thus started what would become a nationwide chain of more than 300 hotels named Days Inn. The Day family eventually sold Days Inn after Mr. Day passed away, but the chain continued to grow and now has more than 1900 locations worldwide serving millions of guests. Because of Cecil B. Day's vision, the landscape of our country was drastically altered. He changed the way millions of people interacted with their families, vacationed, and worked.

We use the word *vision* in some form just about every day.

"Thanks to our visionary leadership…"

"If it weren't for our founding fathers' vision…"

"The company failed because of the limited vision of its leadership."

"He lacked the vision to continue with his education."

Phrases like these pepper our dialogue every day, but we hardly ever stop to think about what they mean. What is vision? Where does it come from? Is it something you're born with, or can you acquire it? It is possible to get it later in life? How is an organization affected by it?

Good questions. And not being able to answer them may very well determine whether you achieve your potential.

I define vision as the ability to look ahead, to foretell your future or the future of your product, company, organization, industry, country, or world. It means having a firm grasp of the principles of cause and effect so that you can accurately predict the likely outcome of a set of circumstances. It is the skill or discipline of predicting future events based on the observation of past or present behavior of subjects. It is the ability to apply these insights to produce a desired outcome or to avoid unpleasant results.

Some people have a strong Power of Vision, but most people don't. Most people have blocked or impaired vision, just like a kid who needs glasses but doesn't know it.

Why People Don't Access Their Power of Vision

If you aren't utilizing the Power of Vision—if you are not able to see that events in your life today are the result of catalysts yesterday, and your actions today will define your life tomorrow—then you would do well to explore the possibility that your vision is blocked. Chances are you have been blinded by an ideal, a value, the demands of the immediate, or ignorance.

Blinded by an Ideal

Few people know what it is to be a professional musician. It's a hard, grueling, and often thankless job. Oh, and it doesn't pay very much either. Because I'm an ex-professional musician, I happen to love musician jokes. There are a ton of them. Here are a few of my favorites.

- How do you know when a drummer is knocking on your door?
  The beat is too fast and he comes in too early.

- What's the difference between God and a rock 'n' roll lead singer?
  God doesn't think he's a rock 'n' roll lead singer. (You might have to think about that one for a minute.)

- What's the difference between a full-time musician and a large pepperoni pizza?
  A large pepperoni pizza can feed a family of four. (That one hurts because it's so true.)

If you don't like those jokes, chances are you're not a musician or haven't been around them that much. But I love them because I can relate to them.

When I worked as a full-time musician, I spent Monday through Thursday in my home office booking myself, talking on the phone, sending out demo tapes, and doing general office work. Then on Friday, I loaded up my van with my equipment, which included speakers (with stands), subwoofer, amplifier, mixing board, effects racks, keyboard (with stand), microphones (with stands), two guitars (with stands), lighting system (with stands), and miles of cables. I might have had more to load, but if I did, I've repressed the memory and don't recall it anymore.

After all the equipment was loaded, I drove two or three hours and arrived at my scheduled event two hours before my performance time so that I had time to set up all my equipment. After I performed for about an hour, it was time to break everything back down, load up the van, and drive the two or three hours back home.

I did this two or three times a week about 35 weeks a year. I also had to produce new music on a regular basis, which meant writing songs, arranging and programming music, and recording the vocals and guitar tracks—all for way less than minimum wage.

Now, some might read that description and think, *That sounds great. I'd like to do that!* And I will admit that there were some good things about living that lifestyle for a while. But I hadn't considered whether it would be sustainable in the long run. Back then it never occurred to me to question whether I would want to live like this for the rest of my life or whether I would physically be able to maintain this lifestyle forever.

I had my first inkling that I might have a problem when I was talking to a pastor on the phone one afternoon about the possibility of playing at his church. He asked some general questions about my career, and then he asked a question that I've never forgotten: "Is this what you're going to do for the rest of your life, Charles?"

Because of his question, I started asking myself some questions that I hadn't really allowed myself to ask before. What would my life look like if I wasn't discovered? (The secret hope of every musician is that the fairy godmother of fame and fortune will tap him on the shoulder with her magic wand.) Did I plan on doing the same thing for a living when I was forty years old? Fifty? Sixty? How long would I have the physical stamina to load hundreds of pounds of equipment each weekend, travel, set it all up, perform, break it down, travel home, and unload? And most importantly, was that lifestyle what I really wanted? Was my real day-to-day experience of being a musician lining up with what I thought it would be?

Looking back, I can see that I was blinded by an ideal that was driven by my passion for music. I had a picture in my mind of what being a musician was like, but in reality, it was something quite different. I let my ideal fill my vision of my future, and that prevented me from seeing where that vision would most likely lead.

And by the way, following your passion is an important element of vision, but as you will see later in this chapter, it is only part of the equation. If you allow your passion for something to overwhelm or replace your critical thinking process, following that passion will become more of a hindrance to your success than a help.

Blinded by a Value

When I first met Edward, my impression was that he was not a very happy person. He seemed to dislike his job, but he had no plans to leave it. He was a pastor after all, and he had been since he graduated from seminary more than 15 years earlier. He believed that pastors are a special breed, set apart by God with a holy calling. You don't walk away from something like that.

In Edward's second year of college, he had a profound, life-changing spiritual experience and decided that the best way he could serve God was to become a pastor. He had been majoring in chemistry before his spiritual awakening but had been counseled that if he really wanted to serve God, he would abandon his dreams of becoming a research scientist and enter the ministry instead. That made a lot of sense to Edward, so he was more than happy to heed the advice he had been given. He eagerly pursued what he had been taught was a higher calling.

The problems started surfacing not long after he accepted his first pastorate at a small Southern church. Edward is not a people person, but he entered a people vocation. Edward is an introvert. He loves people and wants to help them, but he finds constant interaction physically, mentally, and spiritually draining. He is energized by being alone, reading, and researching. He feels trapped by his calling and profession.

My point is not to critique Edward's decision to become a pastor. My point in telling this story is to illustrate the power that values have in our lives. What do I mean by *values*? A value is a belief, a conviction, an ideal that we view as important and use to guide our behavior and inform our attitudes.

In college, Edward adopted a value that restricts his vision to one path, one option, one destination. From his perspective, the only way he can be right with God is to remain on his present course, so any other option cannot even be considered.

I have no desire to dissuade you from pursuing what you feel is your calling. Instead, I want you to consider that if your dreams or ideals preclude your ability to reason, then your vision has become severely limited.

Blinded by the Demands of the Immediate

Trying to live a successful life in this world can be like trying to compose a symphony in a battlefield. Imagine that all your life you've been crawling through a minefield of missed opportunities, bad decisions, and failed attempts. You are now lying wounded in the muddy foxhole of your present circumstances with the bombs of dysfunction and disappointment exploding around you. Your many obligations wage a fierce frontal assault while the consequences of past decisions threaten your flank.

Got the picture? So then, which are you more likely to be thinking when you're lying there—"How do I create a beautiful masterpiece?" or "How do I keep from being blown up?"

Most people usually live in a reactive state of self-preservation, self-medication, or self-indulgence with one goal in mind: survival. Getting by, making ends meet, making it through the day.

All of us are constantly nagged by financial, emotional, spiritual, and physical pressures. Those who bend to the stresses of today and pay attention only to their immediate needs run the catastrophic risk of never developing their Power of Vision.

Blinded by Limited Experience (Ignorance)

Not long ago, a second-year college student named Cathy told me she wants to go to law school when she graduates. I asked her what type of law she wants to practice, and she replied that she wants to prosecute animal-cruelty cases. I asked her if there is a big demand for that specialty in law, and she told me she wasn't sure. I then asked her what activities she would be doing as an attorney, and she didn't know that either. I asked her about the income potential, and she dismissed the question without a thought. After all, everybody knows that attorneys are rich, right?

I continued to press Cathy with a few more questions. Is there any city in the world that has a dedicated prosecutor for animal-rights cases? Are there likely to be any such positions by the time she graduates? What are the hours that an average criminal prosecutor works? How much money does a prosecutor make?

These are all important things to consider when choosing a vocation, but Cathy couldn't or wouldn't hear them because her dream had eclipsed her ability or willingness to reason. Because she had a dream, she wasn't open to an honest evaluation of her plans.

Cathy is not alone in her ignorance. I can't begin to tell you the number of high school and college students I've spoken to who have very definite ideas about what profession they want to enter but haven't researched questions like these:

> **HERE'S A THOUGHT...**
>
> It's hard to focus if you don't know what your vision is.

- What is the average income for that vocation?
- Is the return on investment recoupable? (During the recession of 2009 and 2010, thousands of people piled on the student loans, only to graduate with plenty of debt and no job prospects on the horizon.)
- What lifestyle would that vocation require? (How many hours a day would they have to work? What city and what kind of house would they need to live in?)

• Would they enjoy doing the work day in and day out?

The funny thing about ignorance is that even though you don't intend to be ignorant, you suffer the consequences of it just the same.

Developing the Power of Vision

I hope that by now you are realizing the scope of vision. It's a huge concept that encompasses every area of our lives, big or small.

Whether you go to school. How you spend your money. Whether you get a tattoo. Whether you smoke. What you eat. How you spend your time. Where you live. Whom you date or marry. All of these areas are directly related to the strength of your vision.

The thought of mastering the Power of Vision can be intimidating, but the good news is, all of us can develop our vision. Can and should. Our lives are gifts from God, but with that gift comes responsibility. It is up to us to figure out where we want to go with our lives, how to invest them, and what we want them to be. Failing to give thought to this area of your life would be a terrible oversight (forgive the pun).

In order to build your personal Power of Vision, you need to…

Discover your purpose

Determine your desires

Discern your tomorrow

Discover Your Purpose

Whenever I ask people what their purpose is, their answers often border on the mundane or the messianic. Either it's "I'm going to get the bills paid" or "I'm going to make sure everyone on earth recycles."

But even more often the answer is "Um, I'm not really sure." I get why this question makes people fumble a bit for an answer. Purpose is one of those things that is hard to define, so a lot of mystery and confusion surrounds the subject.

Several of the books about purpose I've read were based on the premise that you should pray and God will reveal it. I am a big believer in the power of prayer, but I also believe I am responsible to do all I can to work toward solutions in my life even as I continue to pray. You can pray all you want for gold, but unless you move some dirt, chances are you're not going to find it. So by all means, pray that God will reveal your purpose, but while you're seeking God's will, I suggest you move some dirt.

Five Things Your Life Coach Might Not Tell You

1. There is no destination called *purpose*. If success is defined as the process of fulfilling your potential, then as you grow, your direction in life will change as your purpose adapts to your growth. Think of purpose as a process or a journey rather than a place you arrive and camp out at for the rest of your life. Show me a person whose purpose has not modified, altered, and refined in the past 20 years, and I'll show you a person who isn't growing.

2. True purpose is rooted in service to others. A supposed purpose that is self-serving isn't a purpose; it's a pastime or an ambition. The word *purpose* indicates intent from the designer. Life is surely supposed to be enjoyable, but it is most fully experienced in giving of one's self to others.

3. Finding and functioning in your purpose doesn't always mean that you get paid for doing it. In fact, this is one of the litmus tests for identifying your purpose—would you continue to participate in that action even if you never got paid for it? Most purpose-oriented people find a way to work their purpose regardless of remuneration. Those are the ones who usually find success in their endeavors.

4. When you're fighting for your life, purpose is a luxury. Until you settle the matters of food and shelter, your purpose is finding food and shelter. There isn't much honor in going on a purpose quest if you have neglected your first purpose, which is caring for your physical, spiritual, and emotional needs (and those of your family if you're an adult). First make a living and then make a difference. Your first responsibility is to provide for yourself so others don't have to.

5. There are several types of purpose.

- *Organizational.* This is the reason a business or government exists. Although organizations are run by people, they exist primarily as separate entities both legally and practically.

- *Communal.* This is the reason a church, synagogue, club, fraternity, or similar group exists. Although they are certainly organized and may function like businesses, they exist primarily as communities.

- *Personal.* This is the reason you get out of bed each day. It identifies your place and contribution in society.

This book is about personal development, so I want to focus on helping you find your personal purpose. I can't tell you what your purpose is, but I can get you started by telling you where to look.

Following Your Passion to Your Purpose

There are essentially two ways that people discover their purpose. One way is not better than the other, and either way is better than sitting around waiting for your fairy godmother to tell you what it is that you're here for. The first way is to follow your passion.

Take a Couple Pounds of Passion...

Let me begin with a word of caution. Make sure that you do not confuse passion with purpose. They are not the same thing. You may be passionate about something, but that doesn't mean that thing is your purpose in life. Passion is a component of purpose, but it does not comprise the whole of it.

So take a moment, a day, or a year to consider your passions. What do you think about all the time? What do you love to do? What really gets you excited? What makes you want to get out of bed every morning?

Sift with Your Personal Value System...

As you think about your passions, evaluate whether they align with your values. If a passion doesn't align with your values, the plain fact of the matter is that it cannot possibly be your purpose. How could you engage in a long-term activity that directly conflicts with what you believe about right and wrong? Most people do not have the ability to live with the internal turmoil this conflict would produce.

As I mentioned earlier, music has been one of my passions. One of my goals in my early twenties was to find a restaurant or bar that would hire me to play guitar and sing. My mission was to earn some money playing music while I waited to be discovered. I remember one interview I had with a small-time talent agent who placed musicians in airport-area hotel bars and restaurants.

"You're going to like this gig, Charles," he told me. "This is a great way for you to make some money." He told me that he was a musician himself and had worked this same circuit for some time. "There's a lot of opportunity here for someone who knows how to work the room."

As I listened to his pitch, I imagined myself crooning away night after night as people practically threw their money at me. But then he said something that changed the way I viewed this opportunity entirely.

"Your job," he said in a matter-of-fact tone, "is to sell alcohol."

I wasn't sure I had heard him correctly, so I asked him to repeat himself.

"Your job is to play songs that keep people in those chairs for as long as possible. Play the songs of their youth, of their first love, of their first heartbreak. Whatever you do, if you want to be successful, you've got to keep them in those chairs."

"What does that have to do with selling alcohol?" I asked.

"The longer people sit there listening to you, the more drinks they'll order, and the more money you'll make in tips," he answered.

The moment he spoke those words, I knew I wasn't going to be a tavern singer. For one thing, my step-grandfather was killed by a drunk driver. I didn't want to be party to keeping people out drinking as long as possible. In addition, alcoholism is rampant in my family, and I couldn't see spending my time intentionally enabling others in what might be an addiction for them.

This was one of the first times my passion directly clashed with my values. Even back then, I knew that direction leads to destination. If I wanted to live a life that reflected my values, my choices would have to reflect those values.

At the end of the day, it doesn't matter how strongly or passionately you like an activity. If it doesn't measure up to the values you've set for your life, it cannot be your purpose.

Add a Ton of Work

People who choose to explore their passion to help them discover their purpose will very quickly find that passion alone is not enough. All passion must be enhanced by skill and education if you are to serve successfully within your purpose. You might need a four-year degree. You might need to get an apprenticeship in your field of interest. You might need to invest your last dime getting the training you need. But whatever you do, you are going to have to invest in personal improvement if you are to be of value and service to others.

Sometimes, in rare instances, passion, values, skill, and education align so that an individual can make a living serving within what he feels is his purpose. That's a wonderful thing to have happen. But the pursuer of this goal should realize that there is no guarantee that his course will result in financial reward. In fact, I'll go so far as to say if financial reward is your *primary* goal in the pursuit of a particular purpose, you should reexamine the possibility that you have missed your purpose.

Following a Need to Your Purpose

As I stated before, just because you're not making money, that doesn't mean you're not making a difference. You don't have to make a living at something for it to be a valid purpose. I have had the pleasure of meeting countless community heroes over the years, including classroom helpers, church workers, fraternal organization volunteers, volunteer firemen, hospital volunteers, and many others who have been fulfilling their purpose without making a dime.

Then there are the folks who make a living serving a noble purpose but will never be abundantly rewarded financially for their commitment and sacrifice. These people include teachers, school nutrition workers, those who serve the needs of the elderly, those who pastor tiny rural churches, and rural water experts. Want some more? I could go on all day. Soldiers who stand between us and slaughter, policemen who do the same, firemen who rush to our homes whenever we need them…The great majority of these people serve a purpose, and because they want to give and fill a need, they willingly accept the fact that they most likely won't be noticed or financially rewarded, and in many cases, won't even be thanked.

I Saw a Need and Tried to Help

It's unlikely that many of these folks selected their purpose by following their passion. Most of them used the second means of finding a purpose, which is to recognize an area of need and then apply your skills and/or education to help meet that need. People who choose this method of purpose fulfillment look for a way to be useful and invest their lives attempting to help others.

George Mueller (1805–1898) is one of the best examples of this method I can give you. Mueller was a Prussian-born English minister who is recognized by many to be the father of the modern orphanage. At a time in England when orphans were routinely neglected or abused, Mueller dedicated his life and material resources to caring for orphans in Bristol. Over the course of his lifetime, his orphanages housed more than 10,000 children.

The primary reason Mueller chose to spend the majority of his life helping orphans was not that he had a burning passion to do so. Instead of following his passion, he followed his compassion. He simply saw a need and stepped up to provide a solution.

You're Going to Have to Move Some Dirt

Finding your purpose isn't a ten-minute exercise. The important thing about purpose in relation to the Power of Vision is that you begin to investigate the *why* of your life. Why are you going on this journey? It's vital to start thinking about this question so that your life has direction and so that you become cognizant of your value.

After you begin exploring and refining your purpose by investigating "why do you want to be?" the next step in building your Power of Vision is taking a look at your "where do you want to be?"

Determine Your Desires

I'm Not Excited!

I was sitting in one of my kids' duller Sunday school classes (sorry, but not all of them are life-changing events) when a young boy sitting to my right turned to me and blurted out, "I'm not excited! This is not exciting me!" As the class continued, he kept repeating these statements to the annoyance of many in the room.

I found out later that the cause of the child's behavior was a mild form of autism. The funny thing, though, was that in the days and weeks following that incident, I found the child's voice echoing in my mind. *I'm not excited!* I'd laugh whenever it would happen, thinking about how much truth there is in that statement and how that simple thought escapes most people.

How many people spend their lives doing what they don't want to do simply because they have never explored the question of what they really want? Of course, all of us have to participate in tasks that are less than enjoyable, but how many people spend so much of their lives working at these tasks that they never stop to ask themselves what they want out of their lives, their jobs, their relationships, their future?

Surveying the Country

When I first began thinking about the importance of knowing what one wants in life, I made a point of asking anyone I could about it. As I traveled across the country speaking, I informally surveyed just about everyone I met, asking the simple question, what do you want in your life?

The surprising thing was that hardly anyone I spoke to was able to answer that question. They always seemed to run my question through the filter of a lifetime of misdirection and misinformation, answering the question they thought I was asking instead of the one I intended. They usually didn't tell me what they wanted out of life, but rather identified the thing they thought would get them what they wanted. I'd get answers like these: "I'd like to get some of my bills paid down." "I want to retire."

These answers don't represent what the people really want, but the *means* that they believe will get them what they want. See the difference? It's like having an abscessed tooth and saying you want a root canal. Nobody wants a root canal. You want your tooth to stop hurting.

WHAT PEOPLE SAY THEY WANT	WHAT THEY USUALLY REALLY WANT
I want to make ends meet.	I want financial freedom.
I want to be a writer.	I want to spend my time creating. I want to be recognized and rewarded for my creativity.
I want to be married.	I want a soul mate, security, companionship, and commitment.
I want another job.	I want more affirmation, more money, and a different way to occupy my time.
I want a girlfriend.	I want companionship.
I'd like to win the lottery.	I want financial freedom.

Because of my occupation, I often run into people who tell me they want to be a comedian or a writer. During these conversations, I sometimes wonder if they know what they're asking for. I'll use these two examples as illustrations.

I Want to Be a Comedian

That's something I know a little about because I made a living at that occupation for years. Do you want to be alone for 23 hours a day? Do you want to be on the road, away from your friends and family, eating fast food, sleeping in mediocre hotels, for 300 days a year, barely making enough money to make ends meet? That's the real-life existence of most full-time comedians.

If that's not what you want, you don't want to be a comedian. It might be that you just want people to laugh at you and like you.

I Want to Be a Writer

Do you want to sit in a room with a computer for 8 to 10 hours a day, six days a week, grinding out words regardless of whether you feel inspired? Do you want to make less than minimum wage? Do you want to sit at a table in a bookstore, hawking your book while people walk right by you because they don't know who you are? Do you want to aggressively market yourself and your books?

If that's not what you want, you don't want to be a writer. The great majority of professional writers also have day jobs or are supported financially by spouses who have dependable, better-paying jobs.

By the way, when people tell me they want to be writers, I ask questions like these: "Do you write right now? What project are you working on right now? How many words have you written on that project this week?" Most people reply that they are not working on anything at the moment. If you want to be a writer, then write something!

Many times people don't really want to be writers. Rather, they see a successful writer, they like what they see, and they form an ideal based on their impressions of that lifestyle. They see themselves whiling away the day, sipping coffee as bestsellers pour through their fingertips and onto their computer screens.

I'm not here to shoot down anyone's dream. I only mean to challenge you to look underneath that dream and uncover your real desire. Again, it's important to not confuse your wants with the means to obtain what you want. Very often they are not one and the same. The danger is that you might pursue what you thought you wanted (such as having a baby) instead of what you really wanted (such as having a meaningful human connection).

Knowing precisely what you want and exactly where you want to go is vital. Why?

- If you don't know these things, you'll never know whether you're on the right path to get it. It's possible that you're

on the right road, but it's not probable. If you aren't sure
where you're heading, you have most likely wandered off
the path and are now walking in circles.

- If you don't know these things, staying the course when
times get tough will be nearly impossible for you because you
will not be in touch with your desired outcome. If you don't
know the reason to persist, you are more likely to give up.

Breaking News

I was riding the bike trails with my neighbor, Mike, at Fort Yargo
State Park on a beautiful November afternoon in 2008. I hate to admit
it, but Mike must have been in a lot better shape than I was, because
after only five minutes of riding with him in the lead, I noticed that he
was gradually pulling away from me. After 15 minutes, he was so far
ahead that I lost sight of him.

I'm a very competitive person, so I started trying to catch up, ped-
aling faster than I should have on an unfamiliar trail. Racing down one
hill and starting back up another, I rounded a tree and hit a big root
in the middle of the trail. My bike stopped dead still, as bicycles are
known to do when they hit stationary objects, and I went sailing over
the handlebars.

As I sat on the hard Georgia clay, I assessed the damage and took a
quick inventory of my body parts to see if any were missing. It looked
like I had escaped injury except for a few cuts and scrapes, so I hopped
back on the bike and finished my ride, albeit a good deal slower than
my original pace.

The next day most of my body was sore, and I noticed a weird
pinching feeling on my right side whenever I got up or sat down. This
went on for the next two weeks until, while I was trying to reach for
something in the garage, I twisted my rib cage and heard a distinct *pop*
in my side. I knew immediately what that sound meant, having broken four ribs on my other side in a traffic accident some 20 years before.
Once you've broken a rib, you never forget what it feels like.

There isn't a whole lot a doctor can do for broken ribs. You can't bandage them up like you see in old Western TV shows because there is a risk of pneumonia from not breathing deeply enough. All you can do is rest and take pain medication.

The problem was that I didn't have time to rest. It was the end of November, and my December calendar was jam-packed with dates that people had booked long before. They were counting on me to show up and do their programs for them, but with the pain I was in, it was hard for me to even think of doing them.

I went to the doctor and got some medication that took some edge off the pain, but even with its edge gone, the pain was still very much alive and kicking.

My first challenge was the first weekend in December. I had four events, from Friday through Monday, which would take me 7000 miles all over the country. I would have shuddered at the thought of doing these events if I hadn't known that shuddering would have caused me a lot of pain.

I'm happy to report that I made it through that long weekend and the rest of the month without canceling one event. I am definitely not trying to paint myself as a tough guy. Anyone who knows me will tell you I'm not anything close to a Clint Eastwood. Far from it. I don't mind telling you I made it through the ordeal only through constant prayer and the grace of God.

I think my main motivation for not canceling the events was that I knew what I wanted. I've worked hard to build my career and to get where I am today. I had a good year financially up to that point, and I didn't want the profitability of my year to be torpedoed by an injury. My financial goals are tied to my family goals. I know what my family needs, and it is my job to get it for them. To let an injury stop my income and impede my career is to thwart the forward movement of what I want for my family.

That's what knowing what you want in life does for you. Looking at the big picture—where you want to go in life, how you want your life to look, where you want to be—changes your focus. Your perspective changes the way you see challenges. Instead of insurmountable obstacles, you see temporary setbacks. Instead of roadblocks, you see speed bumps. That's why it is imperative that you give long, hard thought to what you want in life. If you don't have a solid idea about where you want to go, you will never make it there.

So now ask yourself what you want for your life—financially, vocationally, relationally, spiritually, physically, and emotionally. Imagine for a moment that you are living the last five years of your life. What does it look like? Are you surrounded with your loved ones? Are your financial affairs to your liking? Are you prepared spiritually for the next stage of your eternal journey? Are you able to give to your community? Are you physically active?

What is it exactly that you want? The more that you ponder these questions, the stronger your personal Power of Vision becomes.

Discern Your Tomorrow

The next step in building your personal Power of Vision is discerning your tomorrow. You explored the *possibilities* of your future when we discussed discovering your purpose and determining your desires. Now, we are going to look at the *probabilities* of your future.

By now, you should be at least considering the possibilities of your purpose and desires. You should have some thoughts about how your life might be used or why you are on this journey. You might have begun to get a couple of ideas about where you want to wind up.

What you may not know is that the whole time we have been discussing your purpose and desires, you have been building your personal Power of Vision. The equation looks like this:

Your purpose + your desires = your vision for your life.

Now the only question is, if you continue as you are today, will you fulfill your purpose and realize your desires? Will your vision come into being? Looking into your future really isn't a magic trick. It's just logic. It's if-then thinking.

Cool Hand Lamont

When I knew Lamont back in high school, he was one of those guys everyone thought was cool. He was one of the bad boys, always out to have a good time, always with a girl on his arm. Lamont knew how to party, and he wasn't afraid to try anything, legal or otherwise.

After being held back a grade or two, he finally somehow managed to graduate from high school. I lost touch with him for a few years after that. I heard rumors about him occasionally getting into trouble with the law. He may have even done a little time in jail. Back in the days before the Internet and Facebook, it wasn't as easy as it is today to find out what happened to high school buddies.

Not long ago, I finally ran into Lamont again. Trust me, time isn't kind to any of us, myself included. But a person who has lived the party life like Lamont? Well, how do I put this kindly? Lamont looked like life had taken him out behind the barn and worked him over with a shovel. He still had that easygoing, nonchalant smile that had melted the girls in high school, but now most of the teeth were either rotten or missing. His face was lined like a Rand McNally roadmap, and he had picked up a few nervous twitches along the way.

The thing that surprised me most about Lamont, though, was that he had grown so little over the years. His favorite conversation topic was how wasted he was at the party he went to last week or how hard he was going to party at the next one this weekend. Still out of work. Still no permanent relationships.

It astounds me that the media can celebrate the Lamonts of the world as if they're free spirits who are marching to the beat of a different drum. All the Lamonts I've known have done nothing but consume—and destroy their health and minds in the process.

These days, whenever I see teenagers partying like there's no tomorrow, I want to take them to meet Lamont. You see, I knew Lamont back in the day. He had passions. He had dreams. He had

> **HERE'S A THOUGHT...**
>
> Before you can see the how-to, you have to see the what-if.

desires. But he never developed his Power of Vision. He couldn't see past today. All Lamont had to do, though, was practice a bit of if-then thinking to see where his lifestyle would lead him.

But if-then reasoning does more than projecting the consequences of negative behavior. It also works with positive behavior. So I want you to think about a few areas of your life to determine whether you will achieve your purpose and receive what you want if you continue as you are today in your actions or nonactions, your good or bad behavior.

Career. If you continue as you are today...

- Will you be able to fulfill your purpose? Is your career in any way in conflict with your purpose? Is what you do for a living a violation of your purpose? For example, your job as a real estate salesperson will not conflict with your purpose of knitting baby blankets for needy babies. On the other hand, your job as a traveling salesperson who logs 320 nights a year on the road will very likely conflict with your purpose of building a stronger family. If that is the case, what steps will you take to correct that situation and get on course toward fulfilling your purpose?

- Will your career allow you to get to the place (of stature, service, community, advancement, or lifestyle) that you desire? If not, what changes do you need to make in your career path that will lead you where you want to go?

Relationships. If you continue as you are today...

- Will your marriage be all that you hope? Is your marriage part of your purpose? Are you pursuing growth in your marriage? Are you and your husband or wife unified in purpose? Is your relationship with your kids in agreement with your purpose? If not, what behavior of your own could you change to begin creating those changes?

- Will your relationships have the intimacy you want? If you are single and you continue as you are, will your present behavior lead to a desirable marriage?

Health. If you continue as you are today...

- Will your behavior (diet, exercise, sleep, recreation, habits) allow you to be involved in your purpose 10, 20, 30 years from now?

- Years from now, will you be able to enjoy the life you've built?

Finances. If you continue as you are today...

- Will your finances enable you to participate in your purpose? Are you attending to your first purpose (providing for yourself and those who depend on you) so that you can pursue a purpose beyond your immediate material needs?

- Will you be able to do what you want? What changes do you need to implement immediately for you to get what you want financially? (Hint: Playing the lottery is not a financial plan.)

Tuning Your Vision

Have you ever heard the expression "Out of sight, out of mind"? It means if something leaves your visual range, you're probably not going to think about it anymore. It's human nature. We are instinctually and habitually visual creatures. When you read or hear the words *red wagon*, you don't visualize the letters in your mind. You likely picture a little red Radio Flyer like the one you had when you were a kid. Pictures are the language of your subconscious mind. We think in pictures, dream in pictures, and even use words to paint pictures conversationally. So why not use this powerful medium to reinforce our vision for our lives?

Years ago I heard about a vision tool called the *vision notebook*. A vision notebook is an album or binder containing pictures that represent your vision for your life. Separated into several different sections—relationships, health, career, finances, and spirituality—each part contains pictures that are meaningful to you and depict your vision for your life.

If your vision for your life is to be an active, vibrant senior one day, use Google to look up pictures of people who seem to embody that lifestyle, print them, and place them in your book. If one of your relationship visions is to give your daughter away at her wedding, find pictures that represent that action and place them in your notebook. If part of your vision is to be active in overseas mission work, find relative photos and put them in your notebook. If your financial vision is to be financially free and independent, place pictures in your notebook that represent that lifestyle to you.

The only qualifier for the pictures in your vision notebook is that they must have an emotional connection to your vision. You want to be able to look at these pictures on a daily or weekly basis and be reminded of the place you want to go and the reason you are on your journey. Remember: *Your purpose + your desires = your vision.* Find pictures that remind you of your purpose and desires and look at them on a regular basis.

When you practice this technique, you'll be surprised how well it works. Things that I had in my notebook five years ago, I've already removed because those things are now reality. I looked at them on a regular basis, and I found a way to make them happen.

Of course, we live in a digital age, so your notebook doesn't need to be paper. You can create your notebook of pictures in a file on your computer. The only downside of this method is that your notebook could easily fade from use. You need to place it where you will see it every day. With a paper notebook, I encourage you to place it where you have to physically bump into it or trip over it every day. Of course, you can configure a digital notebook so that you bump into it every day too. The important thing is to be sure that you see it on a regular basis so your mind can absorb the images. The more your mind sees these images, the more you are reminded of where you want to be and why you are on your way.

POWER OF VISION APPLICATION QUESTIONS—
Cleaning Your Windshield

1. Name three of your passions that you could use to serve people.

2. What skills or education do you need to acquire in order to help you live your purpose?

3. Write down three desires that are important to you.

4. If you continue as you are today, are you likely to fulfill your purpose and get what you want in life? What do you need to change in order to make those things happen?

GROUP DISCUSSION QUESTIONS

1. What areas of your life (such as marriage, school, career, or faith) lack vision?

2. What areas of your life are you letting lead themselves rather than envisioning what you would like them to look like?

3. If you change nothing in your life, in five years you will be at essentially the same place in life. In what area(s) of your life would this be unacceptable for you?

3

The Power of
MIND

In the 1997 blockbuster *Men in Black*, Will Smith plays James Darrell Edwards, a street-smart cop who is recruited by a mysterious, covert government agency. Since the first time I saw this movie, one scene in particular has resonated with me.

James is ushered inside a secret government facility to undergo a battery of tests as part of the application process. In the first test, several job applicants sit together in uncomfortable egg-shaped chairs, attempting to fill out test booklets. As each candidate squirms in his chair, struggling to find a surface suitable for writing, James notices an unused coffee table at the center of the room. He walks over to the table and drags it across the floor to his chair. The metal table screeches loudly on the floor, and all the other applicants glare at James as he happily sits back down in his chair and proceeds to fill out the test.

James has solved the puzzle and passed the test.

Why is it that some people think differently than the rest of the pack? Why are some people able to create solutions that haven't occurred to anyone else? What does it take to be that one person in the room who is able to put together the puzzle pieces and find the answer that eludes everyone else?

The Onboard Navigational System or GPS of Your Success Vehicle

I'm on the road a lot, traveling to places I've never been before, so I pretty much live and die by my GPS. It's amazing how quickly we all adapt to new technology. Not long ago I had to navigate my way to each event using only a map and some directions mailed to me by my host. Most of the time, that method worked out decently, but there were other times that it almost turned out disastrously.

About 15 years ago, I was booked to speak at a hospital somewhere in southern Kentucky. It took me a while to drive up from Atlanta, so when I arrived in the area, the sun was setting and it was starting to get dark.

As I made several turns off the interstate, I found myself struggling to see the print on my directions. The farther along I went, the more rural the roads became with fewer street signs and landmarks. After a while, I turned left onto a gravel road, which didn't surprise me much because rural event centers are often located off the beaten track in rustic settings. I remember waving to a group of construction workers off to my right as I drove down the lonely road. They waved back, and I kept going.

After about a mile, I noticed the road getting a lot rougher as it climbed higher and higher. It was darker now, and I was surrounded by nothing but wilderness. I was getting nervous and decided to go back, but I didn't see a place to turn around. I rolled down my window and stuck my head out to check out the road, and what I saw made my blood run cold. There in the dusk, I could barely make out the road, falling off steeply to my left into a dark abyss. I learned later that this was a treacherous and dangerous logging road. Sweating every inch of the way, I managed to retrace my steps and get back down the mountain.

I made it to my event and had a great program, but I still get a sick feeling in the pit of my stomach when I think about how close I came to driving off the side of a mountain that night.

A GPS is designed to keep you out of situations like that. Of course, you still have to use common sense, but most of the time a GPS will help you avoid obstacles and get where you're trying to go. I suppose a GPS can seem magical to a small child or someone who hasn't been exposed to modern technology, but there is nothing magical about it. It relies on the correct programming from its designer and proper input from its user. Without those two pieces of the puzzle, the GPS won't do its job.

How well you navigate around problems and challenges in your life will depend on the strength and programming of your mind.

A Computer Named Dexter

When I was a boy, my parents took our family to see the Disney film *The Computer Wore Tennis Shoes,* which starred a young, up-and-coming actor named Kurt Russell. Russell plays Medford College student Dexter Riley, who gets shocked while tinkering with the school computer. Afterward, he finds that his mental abilities have increased exponentially so that he is able to remember everything he reads. He soon leads his college team in competitions against other colleges on a televised quiz show. Eventually, a blow to the head returns him to his normal level of intelligence.

As a kid, I thought it would be cool to have a superpowered brain and be able to recall every fact I've ever heard. I knew the ability to recollect information is great, but I didn't realize that information by itself doesn't do you much good. If you're going to be successful in life—if your brain is going to help you navigate through obstacles and arrive where you want to go—you're going to need the proper programming too.

The Computer Wore Kmart Tennis Shoes

In my seventh-grade year, my mom and teachers thought it would be a splendid idea to get together and have a meeting to discuss my miserable grades. I didn't know anything about the meeting until it had taken place and my mom cornered me with the news that she and my teachers decided I was way smarter than my grades indicated. In fact—and this is the part that mystified me back then and continues to confound me to this very day—all parties involved agreed that I was intentionally pulling the wool over the teachers' eyes, that I was actually playing dumb so I could slack off. One of my teachers uncovered my alleged scheme by observing that I had a habit of asking intelligent questions in science class.

I was pretty offended at this notion because I knew I hadn't been faking my bad grades. I had really earned them! But what I thought didn't really matter. My parents' and teachers' minds were made up. No more trickery from me! They were on to me now, and by golly, things were going to change. And change they did.

The first things that changed were my parents' and teachers' expectations. All the adults in my life started treating me as if I were an incognito genius, and they took every occasion to remind me that I wasn't going to fool them anymore.

The next change was that my mom and dad leaned heavily on me to make sure I completed every assignment and learned every lesson. They suddenly became involved in my education and threatened dire consequences if I didn't measure up scholastically.

As a result, weird things started happening. I began getting A's in my classes. My teachers took note and patted themselves on the back for foiling my devious plan to fool them all. A few of my fellow students noticed my improved grades, and I saw something in their eyes that I hadn't noticed before—respect. My math teacher even invited me and a handful of other students to visit a brand-new college computer center, back when computers on college campuses were new and novel. I felt just like Dexter Riley.

Unfortunately, this educational experiment lasted only about a year and a half. For some reason, the pressure to excel evaporated once I established that I was capable of getting better grades. Like Dexter Riley, I turned back into a regular kid, and mediocre grades once again dominated my report card. But the lesson I learned through the experience stayed with me over the years: My mind is a powerful thing, and if given the proper treatment, it is capable of performing amazingly well.

Yes, improving my study habits was a very important part of my transformation. But just as important, and maybe even more so, was the fact that I changed the way I thought about myself. I changed the way I perceived my chances of success. Instead of thinking of myself as a subaverage student, I began to think of myself as an above-par student. I learned that the proper programming of my mind leads to a vast improvement in my circumstances. In effect, I learned that I could bend reality.

Bending Reality

Until that point in my life, in my version of reality, I was a slacker. I was on the bottom of the social scale in junior high school. I was poor. I wasn't cool. All in all, I was the very opposite of success. I was mediocre.

And as far as I knew, that was who I was. I had no indication from anyone that I was anything but mediocre, so why on earth would I believe differently? But then came the parent–teacher conference, and my life changed—for a little while at least. My reality wasn't entirely transformed, but I was able to bend it just a little.

Does the phrase *bending reality* sound too much like science fiction for a book on personal development? I don't think so. I think it pretty much sums up what happens when the Power of Mind is employed. Reality is chugging along in one direction. Then somebody gets an idea, and his world or the whole world is changed so that it flows in a different direction than it would have had the idea not come along.

Have you turned on the radio lately? If so, there's a good chance you heard the radio station play a hit song or two. And thousands and thousands of people were probably listening to the same song at the very moment you were. All of you were singing along with the song, note for note, word for word.

How does that happen? Well, a songwriter is going through his day somewhere, and out of nowhere, a catchy phrase and/or tune pops into his head. He then spends the next three hours, three weeks, or three months finishing that song, either by himself or with a group of other songwriters. A demonstration recording is then made and presented to an artist or producer. Paperwork is exchanged and signed, and rights to that song are secured if the songwriter isn't already under contract with a recording company. After that, someone writes a score or chart of the song, and recording sessions follow. The song is then marketed to radio stations, who give the song airplay. Finally, you are driving around singing the same song that the songwriter heard in his mind. He created something and made it part of your existence.

Because of a thought, that songwriter caused the world to change. Maybe the change is minor and goes unnoticed, or maybe the song effects huge change. Maybe because of that song, someone offers a marriage proposal, someone quits her job, someone runs for office, or someone has the courage to keep trying. Because of that song, reality, for countless people, changes just a bit from what it would have been if that song had not been written.

That's the way it works with other things too.

A similar scenario is repeated a thousand times in a thousand different ways in your life every day. With every product you use, every building you enter, every vehicle you pass, every book you read, every movie or TV show you watch, your reality is being bent, molded, shaped by your thoughts and the thoughts of others.

There are those who don't believe in reality bending. They believe the world is how it is and that it will evolve however it is going to evolve. They believe that whatever is going to happen will happen and that we have no say in the course and direction of our lives or the world.

Recently I've been reading about the residential parenting program at several women's correctional institutions around the country. This program allows select, qualified women who are pregnant at the time of their conviction to give birth to their babies and raise the children in prison for a select amount of time—from 30 days to three years, depending on the institution, or until the prisoner's release, whichever comes first.

When I first heard about this program, I was intrigued by the implications. For up to three years, an inmate's child will grow up in a prison environment, sometimes looking out through prison windows at prison walls and razor wire. The child's first hours, days, months, or years will be spent watching Mommy interact with prison guards and other prisoners.

But what if the amount of time a child can spend in prison lengthens in the future? It's not that far-fetched of an idea. It's already a reality in other parts of the world. Mexico, for example, allows children to remain in prison until they are six years old.

But if six years old, why not seven? Why not eight? Why not twelve? Who is to say how long a child can spend in a prison environment without being adversely affected? But my purpose here is not to debate the merits or shortfalls of such a system. I only mention it so that I can ask a couple of questions.

First, if you spent your whole life in prison, how would you know you were in prison? Wouldn't you insist that your life was normal because everyone you knew lived the same way? Wouldn't you define freedom by what you personally experienced your whole life? Apart from books or television, would you even think to question your definition of normal, or would you take for granted that the world was just as you perceived it to be?

And second, are you now living in such a prison? I don't mean this in some weird, esoteric, Matrix-like way. I simply want to know whether you have allowed yourself to consider for a moment whether the way you think about the world is absolutely correct. Do you assume that because of your experience, you know the laws of the universe—what can be done, what is possible, and what isn't?

Show me an entrepreneur who has successfully started and run a business, a pastor who has watched someone's life transform, or an artist who has used his medium to provoke thought, and I'll show you someone who believes in bending reality. If you're trapped in a prison of preconceived notions of what can and cannot be, consider this. There are people all around you who share your prison, but there are also people out there who have jumped the walls and made their escape.

We Interrupt Your Regularly Scheduled Programming

There is no question that we all are being programmed and have been from the day of our birth. People in authority, such as our parents, teachers, and older siblings, contribute to this programming. So do our peers or people groups. The loudest, most insistent, and perhaps most powerful programming we receive, though, is from the media.

Madison Avenue advertising folks are highly skilled at this. They practice it every day without our knowing it.

Not long ago my wife told me she had been craving a Mello Yello soft drink. She hadn't had one in years and was suddenly possessed with the urge to get one. I asked her why she wanted one so suddenly, and she replied she didn't know. I asked her if she had heard or seen a commercial for it anywhere, and she said she hadn't.

When she was taking me to the airport later that week, as she does just about every week, I pointed out several billboards on our route advertising Mello Yello, and I asked her if she had seen them before. She laughed and answered that she sees them every week, but that hadn't registered earlier.

Subliminal messages wallpaper our lives and influence us all in a profound way without our even being aware the process is taking place. We see a commercial, a billboard, or a magazine ad but then think buying the product was our idea. We don't realize that our brains store information and then recall it as resource material for future decisions.

Mass-Programming: Dollars and (Lack of) Sense

Toward the end of 2008 and the beginning of 2009, I spoke at a good number of small-business functions, including several annual meetings for chambers of commerce. I have found that talking to leaders of small businesses at chamber meetings is a great way to get a feel for the economy in a particular area or industry. As I went from state to state and town to town, the conversations regarding the economy started to sound very similar.

Nearly everyone I spoke to had the same thing to say about the preceding year. "Charles, 2008 wasn't easy. We struggled a lot and really had to scrape for business. But when newscasters announced in November that we are officially in a recession, the bottom fell out. Everybody stayed home and sat on their money."

I remember that time very well. The fear in the air was almost tangible. People eagerly tuned in to their news sources to catch the latest updates. The more people watched the news, the more frightened they became, the more frugal they became in their spending habits, and the worse the economy got. Fear is a very powerful thing.

I'm not saying that if the media had ignored the bad economy, everything would have been okay. I'm saying that every business-person I spoke to agreed that the consumer fear ignited and fanned by the media made the economy exponentially worse. Economists can theorize all day long about what began the turnaround, but I believe that when most us calmed down and returned to our normal buying habits, things started getting better for all of us.

Out-of-Gas Unreality

We saw another case of the masses being programmed and experiencing the results a couple of years or so after the devastating effects of Hurricane Katrina. With those images still fresh in our minds, newscasters announced that a hurricane was approaching the East Coast just off the South Carolina coastline. They speculated that if the hurricane were intense enough, it might cause a disruption in the gas lines in the Atlanta area, and as a result, we could very well experience a gas shortage.

The words were barely out of the announcers' mouths when the lines at the gas pumps began forming. Almost like a newsreel scene from the Carter years, the cars lined up at the gas station and wound down the street. People filled up both of their cars and then brought their boats and gas cans.

After a couple of days of these runs on the gas stations, can you venture a guess at what the result was? That's right. The gas stations ran out of gas.

The astounding thing in this story isn't that the gas stations ran out of gas, but that the hurricane never hit the coast, so the gas lines were never harmed. Thus there was no natural reason for the gas shortage other than the panic caused by the suggestion that there might be a problem.

Once again, an announcement was made from a source of authority. People believed the information and accepted it as additional or compatible programming in their minds, and then they acted on those beliefs, causing the theoretical to become reality.

The question is, how many times does this happen to us without us even knowing that it is occurring? And maybe more to the point, how many times has this happened in the past, causing us to base our lives on that programming?

Improper Personal Programming

Some time ago, I was talking with my friend Myron on the phone, telling him about a real-estate education product I had recently bought. Not a get-rich-quick program, mind you, but an honest-to-goodness educational tool that could teach real-estate investment. I found the material very interesting and referred to the program during my conversation with Myron. The name of the program caught Myron's ear and he piped up, "Oh, I bought that program!"

"Great!" I replied, "What did you think about it?"

"Oh, all those things are scams," he said. "I never even opened the package. It's sitting in a box in my spare room."

Talk about creating your own reality! Myron decided the program was useless, so he didn't look at the material. Ergo, the material was useless. He was unable to use the very information that he had paid money to receive because an older, stronger program overrode his desire to learn and grow.

I knew a girl in college who also suffered because of poor programming. Tabitha was a striking beauty but could never manage to date guys who were her equal either in looks or character. How many young people have you known that matched this description?

When Tabitha was a little girl, her father constantly verbally abused her, degrading the way she looked, talked, walked, ate, slept, and everything in between. As a result, she grew up with a poor self-image. Later in life, whenever anyone told her she was beautiful, she simply couldn't hear it. The words just didn't compute, and she might as well have been hearing another language. Whenever a nice young man paid her any attention, she shied away from him and gravitated toward the guys who treated her poorly, guys whose "language" more closely resembled the programming she already had in her mind. She had good input coming in all the time, but because she lacked the proper programming, she didn't know how to process it.

It's Not Me, It's You

I've never met anyone who feels that he has been programmed. Let me say it again. I have never talked to anyone who says, "Yes, most or many of my opinions are not my own, but have been programmed in me by media and my people group." Instead, all the people I've met feel that they have arrived at their present mind-sets and opinions by virtue of their own powers of reason. When I suggest the possibility that their opinions, viewpoints, and beliefs may have been subtly suggested to them, they balk at the notion.

And yet practically all of us grant that this is so for a great number of other people. So most of us concede that this is happening but that it's all happening to everyone else, just not us.

Maybe the reason for this is that we think that being programmed turns us into weak-minded drones. We recall Obi-Wan Kenobi waving his hand in front of the trooper, saying, "These aren't the droids you're looking for," and the trooper answering, "These aren't the droids we're looking for." We think of the Manchurian candidate going into a trance and turning into a robot, intent upon heinous deeds. In reality, the programming we receive is a lot less glamorous but just as effective.

Taking Charge of Your Programming

I have several friends who write computer code in the corporate world. Sometimes they are with a software project from its inception. They are on the design team that conceives the program and then begins writing it. On other occasions, they are brought in to help the process along after the project is already underway, refining the program and adding code here and there. And sometimes they are brought in after the program is already being used by the client. Their job is to work out the bugs and help make the program work as it was originally intended.

When I speak of reprogramming yourself, the process I'm describing is probably closest to the second or third way I mentioned. You're going to be adding pieces of code to enhance your thinking, or you're going to be working out the bugs in the code you already have so that you can work the way you were intended to.

The idea of programming one's mind can make some people uncomfortable, but I can assure you, it's not so much a question of *whether* you will be programmed, but only *how* you will be programmed. Will you wander through the world, believing you are immune to the barrage of input that you are daily assaulted with, or will you control the programming you receive?

I cannot say this strongly enough. You are what you eat physically, spiritually, and mentally. Do yourself a favor and take a quick inventory of the things you have been feeding your brain lately. Have you been giving it something solid that will sustain you during difficult times, or have you been feeding it junk food? Have you been getting all your input from the television, or have you read any of it?

You are a sponge. You are a mirror. To a large degree, you will absorb and then reflect the input of your surroundings. Leave your programming to chance, and you risk absorbing and reflecting a limited, negative, or destructive perspective.

But think about this. If inadvertent environmental input can create destructive thinking, why can't intentional input produce positive change in your mind-set and perspective? Surround yourself with motivational, inspirational, positive material and you will become a reflection of those things.

Your Programming Delivery System

So we've established the need for you to take a hand in your programming, but what is the best way to get it done? To me, the question of whether you are a visual, auditory, or tactile learner is secondary to making sure you control the material you ingest. Certainly use the delivery vehicle that works best for you, but I would caution against allowing yourself to believe that watching television is a step in the right direction.

The television can be a source of good information, but it's not the best medium for self-directed reprogramming. The big problem with television is that it spews a nonstop torrent of information, leaving no time for you to evaluate it. Remember, your goal is to employ the Power of Choice and direct your input rather than taking in whatever happens to come your way. Even on the most innocuous of shows, such as history, nature, or animal programs, most of the information goes by your mental gates unchallenged. You are concentrating on the next thing you're seeing rather than reflecting on the merit of the last statement made. The information goes by unchallenged, so your brain is more likely to file it as factual, thus altering your perspective.

Don't get me wrong—I like watching TV as much as the next guy. Just like you, I have a short list of favorite shows that I like to watch, so no, I don't think all TV is a bad influence. But there are better ways to reprogram your mind for personal development.

Actively directing your programming means giving your brain a chance to interact with the information you are feeding it so you can choose exactly what you want to go into it. The best way to do that is reading books. You can take your eyes off a book anytime you choose and think about what you've just read and how it applies to your life. Concepts don't go by undigested. They are envisioned, examined, and then ingested.

I've found the best books for personal growth to be nonfiction books, but I've also learned a great deal from fictional works. I love novels that take me on a growth journey with the protagonist, and many of the principles I hold dear today I gathered from fiction.

A diet consisting of only fiction, though, tends to be somewhat nonnutritious, so I recommend including at least one motivational or inspirational nonfiction book per month in your reading diet. If you're not used to reading nonfiction, consider starting with my favorite type of nonfiction book, the biography. A good biography takes you through the life of someone who has overcome obstacles and gone on to do great things, impacting the lives of others in a meaningful way.

I don't have a lot of time during my typical day to sit around reading books, so I usually read a bit before turning in at night. I've also found that reading inspirational material first thing every morning is a great idea. I guarantee that if you make it your goal to reprogram your mind by reading just 15 minutes of an inspirational or motivational book every day, you will begin to see your life transform.

If you need help creating your reading list, I am constantly recommending books on Facebook and Twitter that have touched my heart, stimulated my thinking, and challenged my character. I also have an entire page on my website at www.charlesmarshall.net that is dedicated to recommending not only books but inspirational movies as well.

By the way, even though I suggest books as your primary programming method, I don't think you should abandon other programming methods. Hundreds of movies that inspire and uplift are available in every category imaginable—sports, music, arts...you name it. Music can also be a source of inspiration, but again, you have to mind the mental gate. You can't expect to listen to songs about love gone wrong for 16 hours a day and then have a healthy attitude about relationships.

On the other hand, when you take care to actively monitor your input, you will find that immersing yourself in materials with an uplifting perspective will have an immediate positive effect on your outlook.

Of course, there may be additional work to do as well to change your perspective. If you're chronically depressed or if you had an abusive childhood, it's a good idea to look into some professional counseling by a qualified therapist. That therapist will no doubt have you do some serious work to change destructive programming, and some of that work will no doubt include, you guessed it, reading.

Let the Reprogramming Begin

In the mid-1980s, I was a guitar teacher in a music store. I found that teaching someone who already played the guitar was more difficult than teaching someone from scratch. The person who already played guitar had to unlearn his bad habits.

Time after time, I would teach a student a new way to finger a chord on the fretboard, only to have that same student return the next week using his old fingering. Sometimes the student would simply claim he had forgotten to look at his lesson and accidentally slipped back into the old way of playing the chord. Sometimes though, the student would argue that because he already knew and had used the old fingering, he was more comfortable with it. Thus he would deduce that his old way of playing the chord was better than the new way I was recommending.

Reprogramming yourself is a difficult thing to do because it is so uncomfortable. Everything in you screams and begs for the old way even though it is getting you nowhere and could be killing you. Still, you often find yourself making excuses so you can quit and retreat back to the familiar.

The trick to successful self-reprogramming is to remind yourself why you are doing it—focusing on where you want to go and why you want to be there. Sound familiar? I asked you to think about these things when we talked about the Power of Vision. Now I'd like those images in front of you on a daily basis so you'll have the necessary motivation as I challenge you to place your fingers differently on the fretboard.

Looking for Option X

I mentioned earlier that I was occasionally a great student. But far more often, I wasn't. I was often a nervous wreck on test day because I was usually unprepared. Through experience, I found that the worst test question you can have when you haven't studied is the essay question because you have to create an answer out of thin air. I hated essay questions.

At the other end of the scale lies the multiple-choice question, which I consider the friendliest of all test questions. The test asks the question and then quite considerately suggests four or five answers. Sometimes I think the only way I made it through high school was because of multiple-choice questions. Whenever tests were passed out and I saw that the majority of the test consisted of multiple-choice questions, boy, did I breathe a sigh of relief. I knew that even if I didn't have the slightest idea what the answer might be, I still had a 25 percent chance of guessing either A, B, C, or D (all of the above) and getting it right.

Sometimes the teacher got tricky though, adding option E (none of the above). This eliminated the whole advantage of the multiple-choice question by requiring you to know at least a little bit about the subject matter.

It's great when life hands us multiple choice questions. Drive to work or take the bus? Wear short sleeves or long sleeves? Window seat or aisle? Coffee, tea, or soda? But often, it's not that easy. Many times in our jobs, relationships, health, and finances, the answer is E (none of the above). And when that happens, you have to come up with another alternative. Life suddenly turns from a multiple-choice question into an essay question.

In such situations, you want to have studied for the test. You want to have programmed your mind to automatically look for what I call Option X, the answer that's not on the test paper, the answer that isn't obvious.

Problem Solvers' Core Programming

Every creative problem solver I've known or read about is an Option X thinker and has two postulates firmly engrained in his psyche.

1. Every problem has a solution.

If you're going to find the answer to your problem, you have to believe that one exists. If you don't believe the answer exists, you will either deliver a halfhearted effort in looking for a solution or you will walk right by the answer, not seeing it because you were blinded to the possibility of its existence.

Sometime around the middle of 2007 I hired a publicist to promote an inspirational humor book and a comedy DVD that were due to come out in 2008. Because I had two products scheduled to appear in bookstores around the same time, I thought it would be a great opportunity to get as much exposure as possible using the momentum of two new products rather than just one.

The publicity firm I hired was a small boutique company that had been recommended to me by someone I trusted. I signed a one-year agreement with a monthly payment. In return, the publicist, whom I'll call Roberta, assured me that she would work diligently to procure media interviews for me to promote my products.

After the first few months went by, I asked Roberta how the publicity campaign was going and she told me that things were moving along nicely, that we were in the preparation stage, gathering the names and contact information we would need later. Over the next few months, we had several more similar conversations in which I asked about our progress, and she insisted that the wheels were turning, but she was never very specific about what was being accomplished. The more I talked to her, the more I was convinced that I was getting a lot of clouds and wind but no rain.

After about ten months, with the release date for both products rapidly approaching and almost no media interviews to show for my investment, I got a call from Roberta saying our chances of getting any publicity for my products looked pretty hopeless.

Shocked that my publicist would take my money for ten months and then say such a thing to me, I asked her, "What do you mean? How could this be?"

"Well, I've been talking to a lot of other publicists, and the thing we all are seeing is that unless you're talking about the economy or election," (remember, this was 2008), "nobody in the media wants to talk to you."

That didn't sound right to me for a couple of reasons. First, some media might be preoccupied with a subject, but that doesn't mean all the media in the world are. And second, I hadn't been doling out cash for ten months to get to the finish line and have my business partner throw her hands up in defeat.

But the more I spoke with her, the more I realized I wasn't going to change Roberta's mind. She didn't believe an answer existed for the problem, so for her, the problem was insurmountable. She had created her own reality and was attempting to bend my reality as well.

I got off the phone with her and quickly spoke with my board of advisors. After conferring with them, I made the tough decision to buy my way out of the remainder of the contract. I would pay her the rest of what I owed her for the full year but sever my relationship with her two months early. Our thinking was that it was just too dangerous to continue to have her on my team. A negative, unproductive team member can do just as much damage to a business as an intentionally destructive team member. We agreed that my money was already lost because she had practically told me that she was planning on producing no results.

I immediately began researching other public relations companies and found another small firm, owned by some folks who seemed to have an aggressive, positive attitude. Within the first two weeks of my association with them, they had secured about seven or eight television and newspaper interviews.

The two PR firms were approximately the same size with about the same amount of experience. One believed the task was possible. The other didn't. They both got the results they believed they would.

You won't find an answer if you don't believe it exists.

2. *There is always another way to do it.*

If the first way you tried didn't work, try something else. People who try one thing and then give up are what I call *first-barrier thinkers.* First-barrier thinkers hit the first obstacle in problem solving and turn back. I can't tell you the number of times I've had (former) employees come to me after I've assigned them a task and tell me the task wasn't possible, or they couldn't solve the problem, or they tried but couldn't find the answer. They reviewed the multiple-choice questions, circled E (none of the above), and thought they had completed the test. But in real life, E (none of the above), doesn't cut it. If you are to do your job, complete your mission, and have a successful life, you are going to have to find Option X.

When I was a kid, we used to gather around the TV to watch a weekly wildlife program called *Mutual of Omaha's Wild Kingdom.* The show was hosted and narrated by Marlin Perkins, who traveled the world chronicling the challenges of endangered wildlife. Sometimes, Marlin was assisted by Jim Fowler, whose job description seemed to be jumping out of Jeeps that were going 40 miles per hour to tag the ears of dangerous wild animals.

These animals were tagged so they could be identified and tracked for future research. We humans don't need our ears tagged in order to be identified. We identify ourselves with our words. First-barrier thinkers are easy to spot because they constantly pepper their language with phrases like "That won't work," "It costs too much," "You can't do that," and "We tried that."

Whenever successful creative problem solvers hear these words, their programming instantly kicks in, and they discard such words as irrelevant. A quiet voice in their heads answers all the naysaying: "Maybe that's true for you, but I haven't taken a crack at it yet." They know that even though someone has tried solving a problem once or twice and failed, the issue is not necessarily dead.

> **HERE'S A THOUGHT...**
>
> Every barrier to success is just a riddle waiting to be solved.

Today is a new day with new knowledge and resources available. Problems that were unsolvable yesterday may well be solvable today.

Program Yourself to Ask

One of history's most prominent illustrations of Option X thinking is found in the legend of the Gordian knot. The legend goes that an oracle in ancient Phrygia foretold that whoever was able to untie a certain intricate knot tied by Gordius, their king, would be their new ruler.

Years and years went by as many people tried to untie the knot, but all were unsuccessful until about a hundred years later, when Alexander the Great visited the city. Alexander was in dire need of an omen to validate his mission to conquer the known world. At the ripe old age of 23, he was yet undefeated militarily, but he also had not yet scored any decisive victories.

In one version of the legend, Alexander studies the knot as a curious group of spectators forms. Becoming frustrated in his attempts, Alexander is said to have asked, "Does it matter how I do it?" Receiving no definitive answer, Alexander then pulls his sword and cuts through the knot.

A lot of speculation surrounds the legend. Some think that Alexander deduced that the puzzle was unsolvable—that the ends of the rope had been spliced together so they couldn't be untied. Some think he didn't cut the rope at all but instead pulled out its anchor pins, revealing the loose ends of the rope. But nobody argues against the decisive creativity with which he solved the problem.

Personally, I think he found success because he focused on solving *his* problem more than he focused on solving a rope puzzle. His problem was figuring out how to conquer the known world; therefore, the rope puzzle was merely a minor obstacle in the path of his objective. He was clear in his Power of Vision. He knew what he wanted and where he wanted to go. Then he exercised his Power of Mind, finding a way to navigate around the roadblock of omen fulfillment.

What's So Important About a Question?

I especially like one part of Alexander's problem-solving process: asking a question. The question is one of the most powerful tools in the universe. A question can unlock a door, open up a mind, and solve a problem. A good question and Option X are best friends.

Whenever associations or corporations book me to speak at one of their events, one of the first things I do is send them a questionnaire. The purpose of the questionnaire is to educate me about my host's event so I can provide a customized program. The more information they give me, the better job I can do in customizing their program.

One of the most helpful questions I ask on my questionnaire is based on a technique I learned from my wife. Laura spent five years as a features writer for a local newspaper, and she made a habit of asking one final question at the end of each interview: "Is there anything else you'd like to add that I haven't asked you about already?" Laura told me that many times, when she thought she had squeezed every bit of relevant information from the person she was interviewing, this one question would open up a completely new stream of dialogue. Very often the information it produced would turn out to be the most exciting or important part of the interview.

So at the end of my questionnaire, I ask, "Is there anything I've neglected to ask?" I've found that by training myself to ask this question anytime I'm preparing for an event, forming a marketing plan, planning a vacation, or anything else that requires a bit of problem solving, I am opening myself up to solutions beyond my own knowledge, experience, and expertise.

If you can train yourself to master the art of the question, worlds will begin to open up to you. Ask your questions wherever you can, to whomever you can, and by whatever means available.

We truly live in a different world than we did even just a few short years ago. Almost any question you can think of has been addressed on the Internet. Chances are there are how-to videos posted on You-Tube. Or if you prefer, you can post the question on your Facebook page. Our technological age leaves almost no excuse for ignorance—or for not pursuing your goals.

Want to start a business? Somebody has posted something about it.

Have a dream to travel the world on a budget? You can find videos about how to do it.

Need help negotiating your way through a health crisis? There are most likely other people talking about the same affliction online right now.

What Else Should I Program?

As with the Power of Choice, your options for programming yourself are limited only by your own creativity. But also as with the Power of Choice, I have a few ideas for you.

Program a healthy attitude.

I've already hammered this point, so I'll be brief here. Take every chance to embed yourself with positive, uplifting materials—books, articles, movies, whatever. There is too much coming at you on a daily basis not to be proactive on this point. The barrage of negativity you receive on a daily basis can be crushing and overwhelming. Why not take matters into your own hands and decide to give your healthy attitude a little support? The more material you give your mind and spirit to fight with, the stronger you'll be.

Program yourself to innovate.

When I was in second grade, my teacher assigned my class to create our own science project. Like most kids at that time, I went straight to the *World Book Encyclopedia* to search for ideas. After a while, I spotted a scale that looked like it was within my ability to build. My chief obstacle was that my family was poor, so I had no building materials or tools with which to create my project. But even at that young age, my financial situation taught me a valuable lesson. I was learning to innovate. I looked around my house and yard, gathered whatever materials I could, and pieced together my small scale.

I have to admit my little project looked pretty ridiculous sitting next to the polished projects built by my classmates—two small pieces of wood joined by a nail, creating the fulcrum and beam, and two pieces of plastic tied with string serving as the pans. Suffice to say, I was pretty humiliated by my efforts—until the teacher and one of my classmates and then another began to compliment my innovation. It was one of the first times in my life that I learned that if the perfect materials fail to present themselves, I need to use whatever imperfect materials I have at hand.

You may not have the materials you want, but you probably have something you can use to get the job done. You have something better than the perfect set of circumstances. You have a brain. Use it to innovate your solution.

Program yourself to create.

I believe that we are made in the image of our Creator and that the ability and desire to create are deeply ingrained within us all. As small children, we spent much of our time drawing, building, stacking, painting, molding, planting, and playing. But then one day most of us just stopped doing all of that.

Is it not possible that we can recapture a meaningful part of ourselves by joining in the act of creation? The great thing about creating is that nobody can define your means of creation. You are free to participate in acts of creation in whatever way you choose—write a book, write a song, write a play, build a tree house, design a website, design a postcard, design your backyard, design a hairstyle, create a product, build a model car…the possibilities are endless.

If you are participating in the act of creating, you are not only exercising your mind, you are also exercising your soul. You are stretching a part of yourself that most people lose and never find again

POWER OF MIND APPLICATION QUESTIONS—
Checking Your GPS

1. What is typically your first response when confronted with a seemingly impossible task or problem?

2. When was the last time you created an original concept at work?

3. Name three ways someone else's programming has influenced you.

4. Name one step you will take today to self-direct your programming.

GROUP DISCUSSION QUESTIONS

1. Describe a problem you solved with Option X thinking.

2. Name a problem you let yourself believe did not have a solution. As a group, consider some solutions for this problem.

4

The Power of
ACTION

In the 2002 movie *We Were Soldiers*, Mel Gibson plays the role of Lt. Col. Hal Moore, the field commander in the first major battle between American soldiers and those of the People's Army of North Vietnam. Entering into battle with limited intelligence regarding the size and position of the Vietnamese forces, the US Army walked into a ferocious firefight, incurring many casualties.

The situation rapidly became critical. The Vietnamese soldiers vastly outnumbered the Americans. Supplies were low. Morale was low. The death toll was mounting steadily. Moore realized the battle was lost and the enemy would soon launch another attack in order to prevent any Americans from escaping. So Moore did the very last thing his enemy would have expected. As dawn broke, his soldiers affixed bayonets and stormed the enemy lines. Outnumbered and outgunned, the American forces surprised the Vietnamese and overran their position.

Of course, I love the valor and bravery evinced in this story, but the thing that really grabs me is that Lt. Col. Moore was able to employ the Power of Action when it was most needed.

The Accelerator of Your Success Vehicle

The Power of Action is placed midway in the list of the Seven Powers because it is central to all of them. None of the other six Powers can be engaged without it. You can grip the steering wheel of choice, see your desired destination clearly through the windshield of vision, and program your mental GPS, but if you don't press the accelerator of action, you're not going anywhere.

I have never understood the man who is content to sit in his success vehicle, listen to the engine idle, and never hit the accelerator. He reads the motivational books, attends the personal-development seminars, joins support groups…and still does nothing with his life. He does his due diligence, investigates deals from all angles, and receives input and advice from every expert, but he never signs the contract. He allows himself to believe that activity equals forward movement. So he sits in his garage with his success vehicle in neutral, reading the car manual while listening to the engine purr. Can you think of anything sadder?

I once heard someone say that we judge ourselves by our intentions, but we judge other people by their actions. True words. To the world, you are not your promises or declarations of goodwill. You are not your plans, hopes, dreams, or objectives. You are your actions. You are what you do.

Renowned for His Inaction

Amazingly enough, some figures in history are known not for their actions, but for their tendency toward inaction. I wonder if any commander in the history of warfare has been more hesitant to act than George B. McClellan, Union general during the Civil War.

McClellan was a meticulous planner and expert organizer, but when faced with a tough decision, his feet invariably remained firmly cemented in inaction. When his opponents stumbled and he had the chance to advance, he withdrew. When the enemy was outnumbered and within his grasp, he waited for more troops. Time and time again, when McClellan faced Confederate forces, he overestimated his opponent's strength and opted to do nothing.

He never seemed to feel that he had sufficient resources to attack. He was never quite comfortable in engaging risk. Caution was his hallmark. He was eventually removed from his position, and the war was waged and won by more decisive leaders.

All of us are at war. We all fight poverty, health problems, bad habits, bad relationships, bad attitudes, our pasts, and more. The only question is, do you want to be safe, or do you want to win your battles? You can't be safe and wage war. There is no *safe* in a war, and really, the ugly and uncomfortable little secret of life is, there is no such thing as safety in this world at all. But some people still like to believe there is, so their mission is to avoid risk at all costs.

Two Reasons People Don't Act

If life is war and we're all fighting for our lives, why do some people refuse to step in the ring and fight? After studying this subject my whole life, I've concluded that the person who refuses to act is either too cowardly, too complacent, or both.

When I look back at my life, it's not the times that I tried and failed that I regret, but rather the times I didn't even try at all. The things that make me cringe aren't the times I embarrassed myself by not knowing the answer in school, or when I was turned down for a date, or when I failed in a business venture. The memories that make me shake my head and wish for a do-over are the moments in my life when I could have done something but didn't.

When I look at those times, I see my motives easily fall into the categories of fear or complacency.

Fear

I was a decent drummer in school, and when I applied myself, I was able to excel in the band program. But one of the incidents I am most ashamed of in my high school band days was when I intentionally threw an audition.

Every year, right after marching season was over, each band student performed a piece of music for the band director so he or she could be placed in one of two orchestral bands. The band director graded each student's performance and then assigned that student to play in either the symphonic band (the A team) or the concert band (the B team). Of course, everyone wanted to make the symphonic band, and I was proud to have qualified for it my freshman year. But in my sophomore year, I made a decision that I've regretted ever since. I threw the try-out. I actually tried *not* to make symphonic band. I intentionally didn't play well during my audition so that I could be in concert band rather than symphonic band.

I did it because I was fed up with the hazing I had received from upperclassmen. There were more upperclassmen in symphonic band than concert band, so I reasoned that being in concert band would be a lot safer and more comfortable.

The thing I hate about that episode in my life is that I allowed myself to be motivated by fear and the desire for comfort. When I look back, it's not the actions of the upperclassmen that annoy me the most. It's my lack of action—my not doing anything about it.

Fight, Flight, Or…

I've always heard it said that animals have two reactions when they are faced with danger: fight or flight. But I have observed another much more common reaction to danger in the animal kingdom: freeze. When confronted with a dangerous situation, most animals will instinctually stop all movement, if only for a minute.

It makes a lot of sense when you think about it. In the wild, the eyes of a predator detect motion before distinguishing differences in pattern and color. So if the animal freezes right where it is when it first senses danger, it has a chance of eluding the predator.

Unfortunately, this technique doesn't work well at all in the human world. It didn't work for me in my high school band days, and it doesn't work in my business dealings today. In business, he who does nothing in a time of danger will almost certainly be slaughtered. If the world has changed around you and you don't immediately start evaluating your options and making decisions to change what you are doing, your business will be in great danger.

The business owners or salespeople who see danger in the economy but don't choose to adapt, change, and improve their systems, techniques, and methods are making a decision to lose business.

To choose an action is to choose its consequence. It doesn't matter if you intended or wanted a different outcome. Every action produces a corresponding and proportionate reaction. And inaction in the business world can kill a business. Businesspeople who hunker down, circle the wagons, and try to wait out danger without taking any action to defend their business can expect to see decline and decay.

A Tale of Complacency

I had just settled into my seat aboard a small regional jet connecting from Salt Lake City to Sacramento. The flight was carrying a light passenger load, and all the passengers had boarded. I was on the second row from the front, and the seat next to me was empty. From all indications, it looked like it was going to stay that way, and I couldn't have been happier. If you have been fortunate enough to have an empty seat next to you on a flight, you know that it's kind of like an instant upgrade to first class. I love meeting new people and enjoy connecting with fellow passengers, but sometimes it's nice to have a little more room and relax a bit on the flight.

In the seat in front of me sat a young mother holding her baby, who looked about a year old. Next to her, a 40-something-year-old man slumped wearily in his seat. Unkempt and disheveled, he appeared to have made a few bad decisions in his life.

After it became obvious that no one else was going to board, the flight attendant leaned over and spoke to the young mother. "Would it be easier for you if I could find you a seat with an empty seat next to it so you could put your baby next to you?"

"Oh, yes," the young mother replied. "That would be great."

Then the flight attendant turned to the disheveled man next to her and asked, "If I could find an empty seat for you, would you mind moving?"

"No, that'd be fine," the man answered.

Then the flight attendant turned to me, and I could see that I was about to say goodbye to my luxurious, spacious accommodations. Looking at me and smiling without a trace of guilt about what she was about to do, the flight attendant asked, "Would you mind if he [meaning disheveled guy] moved to the seat next to you?"

What kind of question was that? Of course I minded! My cushy imitation-first-class situation was about to change radically by having another full-grown man stuffed into the seat next to me. But I didn't tell the flight attendant any of that. I just smiled as any good Southern boy would and said, "Sure! Bring him on back! Love to have more company back here!"

After the man was packed into the seat beside me, we started talking about all the usual things that passengers talk about. We introduced ourselves, and he told me his name was Rusty. I asked him where he was traveling from, and he told me he had just attended his father's funeral in Ohio. I told him I was sorry to hear that and asked him a bit about his father's passing.

"He was 85 years old and had cancer," Rusty said, shaking his head.

"Were you and your dad very close?" I asked.

"No, we sure weren't," he answered.

When I asked why, I learned that Rusty had been an alcoholic since he was 13 years old. His father's disappointment in him had been deep and had resulted in much conflict over the years. Many Thanksgivings, Christmases, and birthdays had ended in shouting matches and slammed doors. Many times his parents' hopes had been raised with a temporary sobriety, and just as many times their hopes had been crushed with his return to the bottle.

At his father's funeral, his elderly mother pleaded with him to get some help and make the changes his father had longed for him to make.

"Do you have any other family?" I asked, wanting to take some tension out of the situation.

"Yeah, I stayed with my sister and her family the whole week I was there," Rusty answered. "The whole time, my sister begged me to get some help. She even volunteered to find the best rehab center for me and said she'd do whatever she needed to do to make that happen, even helping to pay for it."

"Wow," I said. "She must really love you. It sounds like you have a great family."

"Yeah, I really do," he said.

"Do you have any family in Sacramento?" I asked.

"No, but I have...I mean, I *had* a girlfriend there. We've been together about seven years now, but I don't think she's going to be home when I get back."

"Why is that?" I asked.

"Well, it's the alcohol. I just can't keep a job. She told me that if I lost one more job because of this thing, she was going to leave me. I lost my job right before I flew out to my dad's funeral, and we had a big fight about it."

"Man, I'm so sorry," I said, trying to commiserate with him. But by this time, another part of my brain was starting to kick in. I love the subject of success and creating positive change in one's life, and I'm always interested in what it takes for a person to take a step toward change and then keep walking in that direction. I wondered what it would take for Rusty to make a change. What else could be piled on to the stack of things in his life that would finally produce a catalyst to resurrect a wasted life and produce positive change?

So I thought I'd just ask him and see what he'd have to say. "Listen," I began hesitantly, "I don't want to put you on the spot, and you don't have to answer if you don't want to, but let me ask you a question. What would it take for you to go ahead and get some help and get off the booze?"

"Aw, I don't know," he said, laughing and shaking his head. "One day I guess I'll have my burning-bush moment."

I had never heard that phrase before, but I certainly recognized the biblical reference. The story goes that Moses was tending sheep when he noticed a nearby bush that was on fire but didn't burn up. Curiosity caused him to go over to the bush to investigate, which resulted in a life-altering conversation with God.

Rusty was telling me that he thought that one day he would have an epiphany. One day he would have a revelatory moment when the truth of his situation was laid out for him in such a soul-baring and compelling fashion that he had no choice but to make the decision he knew to be right. One day he would have all the motivation, finances, and emotional support lined up to take the big step. He believed this burning-bush moment would give him the knowledge and strength he needed to make his move.

I couldn't believe what I was hearing. His burning-bush comment was affecting me on so many levels, I was having difficulty choosing what to say next. I knew that two sections of my brain were being activated. On a deeper level, my pity center was beginning to hum, but on a more surface level, my inner smart aleck was getting a wake-up call.

Trying to tamp down my inner smart aleck as best as I could, I struggled to keep my tone respectful and polite as I asked my next question. "Let me get this straight, Rusty," I began. "You just came back from your father's funeral, at which your mother reminded you of your father's dying wish that you seek help for your alcoholism. While you were there, you stayed at your sister's house, and she also begged you to get help, not only offering to help you find a rehab center but also volunteering to help you pay for some or all of the costs. You're going back to your home, where your girlfriend of seven years has just left you because you lost yet another job due to your addiction. On top of all of that, you were seated one row ahead of this one, but you were somehow transferred to a seat right beside a guy whose job is to travel 100,000 miles a year talking to people about making positive changes in their lives. Do I have that about right?"

"Yeah, that's about it," he said with a sigh.

I measured my next words carefully for a moment but then decided I had come too far to turn back. "If you were to have a burning-bush moment in your life," I said, "what do you think that might look like!"

Complacency Kills

It makes me sad to think that some people just won't employ the Power of Action and do something for their own good. You might argue that in such an extreme case as I just described, the individual is incapable of employing the Power of Action and getting better. You might accuse me of callously demanding that this man simply stop being an alcoholic, but nothing could be further from my intent.

My contention is that everybody has a choice in every situation and therefore has the ability to act. Even though an alcoholic may not be able to rehabilitate himself, he still has the choice to either ask for help or accept the help already being offered. Rusty had the opportunity, resources, and support he needed to act, but he preferred to live in the prison of alcoholism, telling himself he was waiting for some indefinable event to happen.

But a burning-bush moment is wherever you find it. It can be a conversation with a friend, a scene in a movie, a point in a sermon, or a story in a book. It might even be in the very book you hold in your hands. It's really up to you. The thing that defines a burning-bush moment is not the urgency of the message or the saliency of the point being made, but rather your response to it.

To wait for that one special catalyst, some external stimulus to cause you to change, is to hand the Power of Choice over to someone else and not employ the Power of Action. The goal for all of us should be to resist the urge to seek the mirage of safety and comfort and then to step forward and act.

Engaging Risk: But What If We All Die?

One of the ladies in my office came into work one day after watching a TV special about the end of the world. As she told me about the program, I could tell it had shaken her up a bit and that she was looking for some reassurance.

"So, do you think we're all going to die?" she asked.

I might have surprised her a bit when I answered, "Yep."

She sat somewhat stunned with her eyes wide and mouth open, so I continued. "We are definitely all going to die one day. I have never met anybody who isn't going to die."

The sooner you make peace with that bit of information, the happier you'll be. As I said before, there is no such thing as safety, so when your doorbell rings, you can't be afraid to answer it. It might just be opportunity coming to call.

A number of years ago, as I was getting ready to self-publish my first book, *Shattering the Glass Slipper*, I went to lunch with the president of a financial company who had booked me to speak at his company's annual meeting. As we ate, we discussed my new book, in which I debuted the concept of the Seven Powers. He told me that this was exactly the type of information he wanted his employees to hear and asked me if he could order 150 copies of the book for me to sign at the meeting, which was less than eight weeks away.

I thought about it for a moment, did some quick math in my head, and then said, "Sure, I'll have them ready for the meeting!"

I had a few challenges to overcome before I could do that. I had never published a book before, so I didn't know how to properly format one. I didn't have any cover art. I hadn't even written my acknowledgments page at that point. Even so, I was able to get the book finished on time, and everyone at the meeting went home with his or her own autographed copy.

I told one of my friends about the challenge of getting the project completed, and he replied, "Man, I'd be scared to make that promise. What would you have done if you hadn't been able to deliver?"

I answered that I wouldn't have promised if I hadn't been reasonably sure I could deliver, and I would have found a way to make it work because I had given my word. The bottom line for me, though, is that I am not going to shrink from a challenge just because danger is on the road.

Taking Initiative

I would estimate that I've had more than 20 kidney stones in my life. If you have had a kidney stone, you know that it can cause a carpet-chewing, writhing-on-the-ground-like-a-snake kind of pain.

The odd thing about kidney stones is that they don't cause all this pain by passing through your body. The painful part occurs after the stone makes its way into the ureter, a narrow, straw-like tube leading from the kidneys to the bladder. Once the stone is there, the ureter can form a seal around it, preventing any fluids from passing through your system on that side of your body. As a result, fluids build up behind the stone, creating a pressure in your side like none you've ever felt. It doesn't take long experiencing this kind of pain before it dawns on you that an emergency room visit would be a really good idea.

After you are admitted, the ER staff starts an IV and begins pumping you full of saline solution in an attempt to flush the stone out of your body. Now, I am no doctor and have no medical training, so I am not recommending that anyone follow my example or do what I do in the event of a kidney stone. But at the first sign of trouble, at the moment I feel the hint of discomfort in my kidneys, I immediately reach for my water bottle and begin drinking as much water as I possibly can.

I can't tell you how hard it is to drink water when I know that the water backing up behind the stone is causing all the pain. When I feel that pain in my side and I am holding the water bottle in my hand, it takes all my willpower to put that bottle to my mouth. But I've found that the sooner I take action—the sooner that I perform the difficult task—the sooner relief comes to me. Conversely, the longer I wait, the greater the pain I experience.

Things don't get better in this world by themselves. Someone has to do something about the problem for it to be fixed.

Have you ever faced an uncomfortable decision, knowing you will experience pain whether you act or choose not to act? Have you ever procrastinated making such a decision, only to have the problem grow worse? Have you noticed that the problem gets worse while you drag your feet?

> **HERE'S A THOUGHT…**
>
> One of the biggest mistakes you can make in life is to do nothing.

I've known countless people who have let the house cave in around them because they were too scared or too lazy to implement the Power of Action. The secret to the Power of Action is to focus on what you learned as you explored your Power of Vision. Ask yourself what will happen if you fail to act. Are you comfortable with the consequences of your inaction? What will you gain if you do act?

I have found that in most matters (except when you're angry, for acting in anger is rarely beneficial), doing due diligence and then employing the Power of Action are the right steps to take. I have also found that inaction almost always results in disaster or decay.

How Do I Begin?

Writing It Down Makes It Real

If you are ever going to make something happen, you need to write it down. You can write it in the form of a to-do list or a note on your calendar. It can be handwritten or electronic. It doesn't matter. The only thing that matters is that you write it down and put it where you will see it.

Every night, before I go to bed, I make out a to-do list and put it in the middle of the floor so I will literally trip over it the following morning. Old school, I know, but it works for me. In my office, we have notes on calendars, on computer desktops, and on bulletin boards, each with a specific purpose.

> **HERE'S A THOUGHT...**
>
> A plan that isn't written down isn't a plan. It's an idea. It becomes a plan when it's visible.

There is something powerful about the written word. You are sending a message to yourself. A note to yourself demands a response. Either you will make the decision to ignore what is written down or you will do what it says.

Every Action Needs an Appointment

If it's going to be done, you need to put it on the calendar and set a time when you intend to at least begin. The danger of not setting an appointment for your action is that you will wait for "someday" to begin, and someday never comes. People who wait for someday to take a ride in their success vehicle spend their whole lives in the garage.

I'm not suggesting you act in haste or without thoroughly researching your options. But once you get an idea of what you want to do, it's time to set an appointment by writing it down. You don't need to have your whole plan completed before you set your appointment. You don't even need to have most of your questions answered regarding how you are to complete your mission. You just need to set a time and write it down.

You've Made Your Choices. Now Take the Action.

Take Creative Action

Everyone has a song to sing, a story to tell, a picture to paint. Maybe you don't consider yourself very artistic, and that's fine. The question is, are you communicating your message to the world around you? Are you expressing your spirit through the gifts you have been given?

Sometimes that means baking a cake, coaching a softball team, participating in a book club, reading to a child, or singing in the choir. Sometimes it's building a tree house, planting a garden, landscaping the yard, or knitting a hat. It could be repairing bicycles, restoring old cars, or making furniture. It might be anything, but I guarantee you that you have a song to sing. Therefore you have a responsibility to sing it.

I can also promise you that if you don't use your gifts, they will fade away. You use them or you lose them.

Creativity begets creativity. The only way you run out of creativity is to not act on the ideas you have. When you habitually choose not to act on creative ideas, you train your subconscious to not send you any more of them. You are essentially saying, "Don't bother sending me any more ideas. They won't be used." And so the creative part of yourself dries up and withers like an unused limb.

The good news is that the reverse is also true. I know that I will never run out of ideas as long as I continue to act on the ones I have. If I want more ideas in my life, I exercise my creativity, and the flow continues.

Take Relational Action

It's an amazing thing that we know to take our cars to a mechanic for regularly scheduled maintenance. We know to cut our lawns and trim our hedges. We know to continue our education. We know to practice playing an instrument or throwing a ball if we want to improve. But when it comes to our romantic relationships, we have the inane (and media-programmed) thought that they should just happen. We believe that if we "fall out of love," then "it was never meant to be" and that "God has led me to someone else" who is "really the right one for me this time."

To think of any other area of your life that way is ridiculous. "I thought I had found the right car, but after a couple of years it began running roughly, so I realized I had never loved it in the first place. So I left it on the side of the road and found a brand-new car that I'm sure is the right one for me!"

"Did you ever put oil in the car or take it in for a tune-up?"

"No, you shouldn't have to work on a car if it's the right one for you."

Pretty ridiculous, right? What if we approached all our relationships with at least the same amount of common sense with which we treat our cars? What if we knew that once every two or three weeks we need time alone, dating our spouse? What if we just had a conversation—not about the kids, house, or bills, but just sharing something of ourselves?

How does the Power of Action work in romantic relationships if you aren't married or dating anyone and you have no prospects on the horizon? If you're still holding on to a made-for-television romantic notion that Brad Pitt (or whoever the current Hollywood heartthrob is) is going to ride in on his Harley and take you back to his million-dollar mansion, then wake up. Or guys, if you're lying around in your sweats and playing John Madden all day, and you aren't dating anyone because you haven't found a supermodel who wants to date you, please stop living in fantasyland.

If you want to meet your match, go where people are. Not just any people, but like-minded people whom you might want to know better. Then walk across the room and talk to them. That could be a literal room at a social gathering, or it could be a virtual room at a dating website. I've met countless people who met online and initiated healthy relationships. (Fear may have begun buzzing around your mind when you read these words, so let me add that yes, you should be cautious when meeting strangers online. Yes, use common sense and meet in public places at first. No, if you read about somebody somewhere getting in trouble because they met someone online, that doesn't mean that the whole method should be thrown out the window.)

And what if we applied the Power of Action to the rest of our family? What if we (brace yourself) actually spent time with our kids? *Gasp!* After observing successful families for a number of years, I've noticed that the one factor that most influences kids' choices in life is their interaction and involvement with their parents. How relevant are you in your kids' lives? What place do you have in their lives? Do you have a built-in appointment with them to hang out, or are you like ships passing in the night?

Remember, people (including your kids) don't care what you know until they know that you care. Want another saying? How about this—kids spell love T-I-M-E. You don't have the right to gripe about your kids if you neglect to hang out with them. If you are only the big person who comes around about once a day and tells them what they're doing wrong, then you're not employing the Power of Action.

How about this instead. Every Monday (or whichever day is best), you and your daughter take a walk. Or you and your son throw the baseball. Or you go eat lunch. It doesn't really matter what the activity is as long as you make yourself available for dialogue. It's amazing how your kids will ask you questions if you prove to them that you are safe to talk to and open to hearing what they say.

And by the way, watching TV is not spending time together. But you already knew that, didn't you?

Take Financial Action

We live in a time when there is more advice, more information, and more input regarding our personal finances than ever before. You can't watch TV, listen to the radio, or walk into a bookstore without bumping into another guru wanting to talk about your money.

We're told to save, not spend; invest, not consume. We need to make more than we spend, and watch what we buy and how we buy it. So it's not information we lack. It's impetus. Are you applying the Power of Action for the betterment of your household?

But I'd like to visit another area of financial action. Consider the philosophical question, am I my brother's keeper? I believe the answer is yes—if you choose to be.

The true adventure in life is allowing yourself to be part of a miracle in someone else's life. That means applying the Power of Action in responsible giving in your community and beyond. And by "responsible giving" I mean that throwing money at life's problems isn't always the answer. Most of the time that gift of money needs to be accompanied by a fair amount of oversight and accountability. But responsible giving should never be used as an excuse for doing nothing.

I believe it is a foundational life principle that we are placed on the planet not only to enjoy its pleasures but also to be the answer to someone else's prayer.

Take Spiritual Action

I sometimes hear people attempt to object to the Power of Action principles on spiritual grounds. These people believe that taking action is somehow in conflict with a walk of faith. They think that the truly spiritual person will let go and let God, meaning that sitting back and doing nothing is the God-sanctioned method of problem resolution.

I have a hard time with this philosophy, especially considering that every biblical miracle occurred when somebody did something. Somebody stood up, raised a staff, spit in some mud, touched somebody, or got in some water. Somebody took some action. So how can any argument be made for those who want to interact with God by waiting for him to act when they can't be persuaded to lift a finger? Why would we expect him to do what we won't?

There have been other times that I've wondered at the actions some well-intentioned people have taken in the name of faith. Not long ago I spoke to a guy about the giant Gothic cross he had tattooed on his arm. He told me he got tattooed a few years back because he loved God so much and wanted to express his faith. I appreciate the sentiment, but

I believe a better, more relevant way to express your faith might be to paint a picture with your life that positively impacts the lives of others.

Bruce Olson is one of the best modern-day examples I can give you of an individual who embodies this principle. At the age of 19, with very little training or financial backing, he walked into a South American jungle to bring the word of God to the Motilone Indians, a fierce tribe of headhunters known for their inhospitable behavior toward strangers. His initial efforts were less than successful, to say the least, but today he is known the world over as a community leader, missionary, and advocate for the Motilones in Columbia.

When I contrast Bruce Olson's actions in expressing his faith with getting a tattoo, I can't help feeling that perhaps Bruce's life efforts and actions are making a bigger difference.

We live in a society that values intent the same as effect. I am submitting to you that your faith will be better expressed by employing the Power of Action to do something tangible to help others.

Take Physical Action

When I was a teenager, I was six feet three inches tall and weighed 155 pounds. Because I was so skinny, I desperately wanted to gain weight, but even though I ate a mountain of food, I still wasn't able to pack on the pounds. I was active but not especially athletic, so it wasn't as though I was burning up all my calories through physical activity. It was just how my metabolism functioned at that age. I could eat or drink whatever I wanted, whenever I wanted. You name it—Oreos, honey buns, soda, chips, whatever. (Am I the only one getting hungry right now?) I could eat it all, and I never put on any weight or felt any worse for wear.

Fast forward a couple thousand years to my present age, and…well, I'm not a teenager anymore. Things have changed. I can't get away with the dietary behavior of my youth without expecting dire consequences. Oh, I tried for a while when I was in my twenties, but believe me, you can't sneak junk food into your body without the bathroom scale hearing about it. The bathroom mirror either.

Your body is like a stubborn, recalcitrant child. It wants what it wants and will pitch a fit when it doesn't get it. You are the master of your body, but if you don't control it, it will control you.

But we know this. Everyone knows we're supposed to eat right and exercise, but people react to this information in different ways. Some take notice and begin to take baby steps toward treating their health seriously. Others wait until they have a head-on collision and are hospitalized before they put on the brakes.

I'm not a monk. I can't subsist on dry crackers and dehydrated fish. (Isn't that what monks eat?) But I realize that I no longer have the luxury of lethargy. I want to live. I understand that acting to have good health doesn't guarantee that I'll live a long time, but I also understand that neglecting the maintenance of my body will shorten my life span. I am not willing to leverage a day with my family in the future because I want to eat ice cream and donuts today!

Take Occupational Action

I walked into a little shop in an airport and asked the guy behind the counter how he was doing. He mumbled something about being as well as he could be, being stuck there. When I asked him where else he would like to be, he thought for a moment and told me he'd rather be in Alaska. I asked him why he wanted to be in Alaska, and he said it was because anywhere had to be better than working at the crummy job he currently had.

It was like I was talking to myself 30 years ago. I too had been a young man working at a dead-end job. I had no hope, no prospects, and no clue as to how I could change my life. This young man appeared to be in pretty much the same boat. I didn't have very long to talk to him before my flight took off, and I seemed to be an unwanted guest at his pity party. But in the short time I had, I did my best to convince him that he did have options available.

At no other time in history has there been so much opportunity. If you want to do something different for a living, then in most cases, the only thing stopping you is you. Yes, you'll have to do some creative problem solving. Yes, you'll probably have to sacrifice. Yes, it won't be easy, but most things worth doing rarely are.

I don't believe your job is a complete representation of who you are, but you do spend a significant portion of your life working, so why not do something you feel good about? If you don't like the job you're working at, there are three positive actions you can take.

1. Get another one! Take a hike. Take a class. Get some training. Transition yourself into a better situation.

2. Change the job. Know it or not, you have influence. Instead of running from the problem, you can be part of the solution. What can you do to make your workplace a better place to be?

3. Change yourself. My dad used to say, "If everyone else in the world has a problem with you, then it's not the whole world with the problem." As I mentioned in the Power of Choice chapter, your attitude can change the way you see the world. How is your attitude coloring your work experience?

You have to decide for yourself whether to be the type of person who does something about your job situation or the type of person who does nothing.

POWER OF ACTION APPLICATION QUESTIONS—
Stepping on Your Growth Accelerator

1. Describe a time when you have let fear keep you from taking action.

2. Name one time when comfort or complacency kept you from taking action.

3. Write down three actions you would like to begin to implement within the next three days.

4. In what one area of your life do you most need to employ the Power of Action (relationships, finances, health…)?

GROUP DISCUSSION QUESTIONS

1. What idea do you need to act on in your life?

2. What most often keeps you from taking action in your life when you know you need to act?

3. In what part of your life is fear preventing you from taking action?

4. Tell of a time when you employed the Power of Action and share the results (positive or negative).

5

The Power of
FAILURE

///

By the late 1970s, Journey was pretty much finished. The band had recorded three albums, all of which had been critical successes but market failures. They had managed to sell several hundred thousand albums cumulatively, but in the recording industry, selling one or two hundred thousand units per album is pretty much like selling none at all.

At the core of the group were guitarist Neal Schon and keyboardist Gregg Rolie. Neal started his musical career at a young age, joining the legendary group Santana when he was only 15. Years later, after leaving Santana, Neal partnered with his former band member Gregg to create their dream band. In its early stages, Journey was still finding its way, creating songs that featured expert musicianship rather than the song craft for which the band would later be known. The group seemed to have most of what they needed for success, but for some reason, they fell just short of their potential. They were missing some key ingredient.

Meanwhile, in another part of California, a young man named Steve Perry had given up on his dream to be a singer. Steve had been a member of a promising new band called Alien Project, but on the eve of signing a recording contract, his band's bass player, Richard Michaels, was killed in a car wreck. Steve was devastated and decided to quit the music business. He moved back home to work with his step-father repairing turkey coops to pay back the debts he accrued record-ing his demo tapes.

But then Steve got a phone call from Herbie Herbert, the manager of a struggling band named Journey. Herbie convinced Steve to give a career in music one more shot by trying out as the lead singer.

Neal and Gregg met with Steve one afternoon to get a feel for his style and find out what he had to offer. Afterward, Neal told Herbie that essentially he just wasn't feeling it—that he and Greg didn't want Steve to join the band. Herbie, however, had another opinion on the matter. He told Neal that it had already happened and that Steve was now in the band. Done deal. Matter closed.

Fast-forward two or three decades, and Journey has a place with the top-selling bands of all time. Their music is played regularly on radio stations all around the world, and their albums continue to sell at a healthy pace. But none of it would have happened if the principle play-ers had accepted failure as the final stop in their journey.

How many other Steve Perrys are there in the world whose stories we'll never know because they quit when confronted with devastation and failure? What would Steve Perry's life have looked like if he had accepted the defeat that life handed him and refused to forge ahead?

Those who would be successful are never strangers to failure. I challenge you to name one world leader in any area—music, politics, sports, television, movies—who is not intimately acquainted with fail-ure. Winners never get comfortable with failure, but neither do they shrink from it.

People who actively explore the possibilities of their potential are bloodied and bruised, beaten and battered. And all of us are to some degree, aren't we? The thing that distinguishes people in the winner's circle is that they got up again. Some of them will tell you they were just too dumb to know any better. They will quip that if they were smarter, they would have stayed down for the count, but don't you believe it for a minute. All of them have exercised the Power of Failure.

The Emergency Roadside Repair Kit of Your Success Vehicle

What is your reaction when failure knocks on your door? It might be a temporary setback or a cataclysmic tornado that has blown through your life. But whatever it is, however great or small, it *will* knock on your door, and probably sooner rather than later. When it does, how will you react? Will you slam the door in its face in complete denial? Will you let it attach itself to you and follow you around the rest of your life? Will you invite it inside, offer it refreshments, and ask it to stay awhile? How will you respond the next time it shows up at your doorstep? How did you react the last time it rang your doorbell?

Failure can be devastating. It often means the death of a dream and the realization of a nightmare. It's so painful, some people spend their entire lives trying to avoid it. They see it as the Wicked Witch of the West, Darth Vader, and the boogeyman all rolled up in one.

But what if instead of thinking of failure as our enemy, we thought of it more as a neutral force, like electricity, which, if tamed and harnessed, can produce tremendous power? Sure, if you're not paying attention, electricity can bite you or even end your life, but if you know its secrets, it can give you power.

Every car breaks down now and then. Sometimes your car just needs a flat tire changed. Sometimes it has been in a major crash and needs to be rebuilt from the frame up. Setbacks, devastation, and defeat are parts of everyone's journey, so you have to ask yourself what is in your emergency roadside repair kit.

Do you have the right tools to deal with the inevitable breakdowns so that you can continue your journey? Do you have the correct perspective of failure, which will allow you to learn from it and continue to follow your vision? Or do you allow failure to truncate your journey right there on the side of the road? Are you the type of person who stays right where you are when you break down?

Failure may be inevitable, but utter defeat is not. You haven't lost unless you abandon your vision on the side of the road and run for home. Sailors don't give up when a strong wind blows against them. They adjust their sails. They use that wind to help move their vessels forward. They use adversity as a form of propulsion.

The Nature of Failure

Gerald was a good-hearted gentleman whose vision was to hold a community-wide business seminar to encourage businesspeople during the height of the recession in 2009. He found me on the Internet and called one day to book me to be the keynote speaker for his seminar. As we discussed his event, he told me he had hopes of producing a helpful, inspirational event where business folks could be encouraged and get some helpful tips about surviving and thriving in an ailing economy. Almost as an afterthought, Gerald added that he also wanted to make a profit from the event so he could pay his bills and support his family.

As the event date approached, Gerald expressed optimism about having a good turnout. He told me he was primarily promoting his event through a few local churches, meaning he had spoken with a few pastors and they had enthusiastically offered their support. Gerald interpreted that to mean that these pastors would announce his seminar on Sunday morning and encourage people to buy tickets. When I suggested to Gerald that pastors have a lot to do and promoting his event might not necessarily be on the top of their priority lists, he waved off my concerns, telling me he was satisfied that all was as it should be and that he was on track toward having a full house for his event.

A few days before the seminar, a troubled Gerald called, telling me our crowd might be a bit thin.

"How many people do you have signed up right now?" I asked.

"Well, to be honest, less than twenty people have bought tickets," Gerald replied.

He already sounded pretty bummed, out and I didn't want to make it any worse for him, but I thought it might be best if we went ahead and got the bad news on the table.

"Gerald, how many people would 'less than twenty' be?"

He hemmed and hawed for a minute and then said, "Um, well… uh, less than ten."

I said, "Gerald, I don't want to put you on the spot, but give it to me straight. I can take it. Exactly how many people have bought tickets?"

He sighed and said, "Right now, uh…three."

I can't say I was completely shocked. Based on my experience and from what I had heard from Gerald about his marketing efforts, I would have been a little surprised had he been able to fill the room.

I can't tell you how dejected Gerald sounded over the phone. He was shocked that people hadn't rushed to sign up for his seminar. It was such a great idea, after all. Why didn't anybody see that?

There was also an element of spiritual dejection running throughout his comments. He really thought he had gotten the green light from God on this project. He wondered if he missed God's leading. He had prayed long and hard before entering into this venture and had moved ahead only after he felt spiritually comfortable that he was following God's will. Or maybe God had abandoned him, Gerald speculated. He hated to admit it, but part of him felt that he had done everything right, but God had failed to come through for him.

As we talked, I tried to share a different perspective. Maybe there was a less spiritual reason for his failure. Gerald had never run a business before, nor had he ever been in sales. Although he had a heart to encourage people, the project he was planning was a business venture, not a missionary effort. If he expected people to hand over cash for a ticket, he needed to think of this effort as a product to be marketed and sold. Savvy businesspeople don't spend a lot of time hoping their businesses take off. They make sure they do.

This was Gerald's first attempt to market a product, and he failed. He lost the money he had invested in materials and room rental, and he felt he had embarrassed himself in front of his family and friends. He told me he had learned his lesson and wouldn't ever be attempting anything like this again.

It sounded to me as if Gerald had learned the wrong lesson, and I told him so. I told him that all his life until that point, he had been eating at the kids' table. But making the attempt to do something larger than himself, bigger than he had ever dreamed of doing before, earned him the right to sit at the grown-ups' table.

A place at the grown-ups' table has to be earned, purchased with effort, struggle, failure, and pain. Those who work only within their comfort zone, who never attempt something beyond their immediate ability, will never know what it's like to have the right to sit in the company of those men and women who have challenged themselves and embraced risk.

Speaking of Failure

Failure is never kind, but it is always honest. It won't spare your feelings or soothe your ego. It's blunt, brutal, and hurtful. But it's also the best friend you could have if you are willing to put away your bruised ego and humbly sit at its feet.

I didn't learn how to be a public speaker by being in front of friendly, easygoing audiences. I became a good speaker because I've spent a lot of time in the trenches. I've spoken at nursing homes where half the crowd was asleep and the other half was yelling incoherent phrases. I've spoken for junior high school kids who either didn't get the jokes or were too self-conscious to laugh. I've spoken to homeless people who didn't want to be in the crowd and didn't care what I had to say. And I've spoken to a few stuffed shirts who were a little full of themselves.

I've bombed more times than I can count, but I walked away from each of those times wondering what I could do the next time to produce a different outcome. Through trial and error, I learned the best way to set up a room for crowd connection. I learned who to interact with in the audience and who to stay away from. I learned how to tell a joke in a huge, expansive room or a small, intimate setting. And I know I wouldn't have learned any of these things had I not weathered the many, many storms of public speaking.

Storms? It's hard to describe the gauntlet I've had to run to get to this place in my career. I've been misquoted, misunderstood, and maligned. I've had people write me long letters (anonymous, of course), telling me why I am an evil person for telling jokes in churches or why I am a horrible person for telling that one joke in an hour-long presentation.

There have been many times I've pouted and sulked when things didn't go my way. I've wanted to give up and quit speaking and go find something sensible and safe to do with my life. But I never did that for three reasons.

1. I hate failure, but I hate quitting even more.

2. I hate adversity, but I love what I'm doing more.

3. There is no such thing as safety.

Now I know that not only have I earned my place at the grown-ups' table, I truly belong there. Most of the time when I speak these days, I'm speaking to wonderful, open people who love to laugh and want to learn. But on those occasions when I run into a tough crowd, I'm not intimidated because I'm ready for them. Chances are I've been in harder situations before. And if I run into a situation I haven't seen before that gives me trouble, well, I'll sit down and listen to what that failure has to teach me.

Direct Failing Campaigns

When I was getting my comedy career off the ground, I did a lot of direct-mail marketing. This was way back in the dark ages before there was such a thing as Internet marketing. For that matter, it was before there was an Internet. Fortunately, I had some very generous friends who volunteered their time to help stuff untold thousands of envelopes.

On one occasion, I was delivering some brochures, letters, and envelopes to my friend Thomas. Thomas had a landscaping business that wasn't exactly thriving, so he had graciously offered to help me out during his downtime. As we carried boxes of mailing materials into his home, we started talking about how his business was doing, or more specifically, how it wasn't doing. Thomas told me that he blamed the economy mostly for his lack of business, but he also guessed that people weren't interested in buying landscaping services right then. Or maybe they were just happy with their old service. Truth was, he confided, he didn't really know why the phone wasn't ringing.

"How do you get the majority of your business?" I asked.

"I have an ad in the Yellow Pages," Thomas answered, "but it doesn't seem to be working all that well these days."

"Have you ever tried marketing your business any other ways to get more business?"

"Oh, yeah, but none of them worked."

I was pretty amazed at this because I'm a huge fan of marketing. I like the idea of employing the Powers of Choice, Mind, and Action to proactively move my business forward, so when Thomas told me that absolutely no marketing method has worked for him, he really piqued my interest. As we talked a bit more, I learned that he mainly did commercial landscaping, so I asked him if he had ever tried knocking on doors and handing out business cards.

"Sure have," he answered. "I've tried that, but it definitely doesn't work."

"How many times did you try it?" I asked.

Thomas hesitated for a moment and then answered, "Well, I tried it one afternoon, but it didn't bring in one bit of business."

Now the picture was getting clearer. "So you tried visiting businesses and introducing yourself for one afternoon. How many companies would you say that you went to?"

"Oh, about three or four," Thomas answered.

To think of a failure as anything but a first attempt is a mistake. For years, the words "Just once won't work" were written in big, bold letters on the dry erase board in my office. You can't try a marketing effort one time and expect anything to come from it. You can't plant just one seed per hole and expect to have a robust crop. You can't pitch your product one time and expect to retire.

Success is a process, and failure is a key component. Your success doesn't come down to one event, one time, one effort. It is the cumulative result of many attempts, tests, and efforts. If you stop without learning the lessons failure has to teach, you are creating a reality for yourself that will limit you and keep you from the achievement you desire.

Not Exactly Rolling in the (Pizza) Dough

I answered the phone just after midnight and heard the panicked voice of my business partner on the other end of the line. "If you want anything from the restaurant, you'd better come get it now," Frank said. "They're kicking us out of the building tomorrow morning."

"What!" I practically yelled into the phone. "We're being evicted? How did that happen? When did you find out about this?"

"I can't talk now," Frank replied. "But I'll meet you down there in an hour, and I'll explain everything then."

I knew business had not been going well, but I didn't know it had gotten this bad. As I drove to our soon-to-be-former restaurant location, I reviewed the past six months. I had met Frank through a friend during the winter of 1987. Frank enthusiastically pitched me on the pizza restaurant he had recently opened. He was looking for investment partners, and I was flush with cash from a recent insurance settlement.

A fool and his money, huh? I couldn't have been more unprepared for Frank. I was in my midtwenties and had never seen a business proposal until I saw his. I had no idea what one was or how to read it. But Frank talked a good game, and soon I was handing over a check for the better portion of my savings account. After knowing him for only a few weeks, Frank and I were in business together.

As I got to know Frank and saw how he ran his business, I gradually came to realize I had made a mistake. I started helping out around the restaurant in any way I could in my spare time. I learned to make pizza. I waited tables. I even delivered pizzas a couple of times. Anything to help out. I was a free, highly motivated labor source.

When the phone isn't ringing and no one is coming in the door, desperate entrepreneurs often start making desperate decisions. I saw Frank begin to make wild, Hail Mary marketing moves. One local printer offered to print 10,000 fliers and personally distribute them to every student on campus at a local college. Frank jumped at the proposal, only to later find out that instead of delivering the fliers, the printer left stacks of them in dormitory lobbies and considered his obligation fulfilled. We got about a half-dozen orders from the effort but lost too much money in the process.

Things went from bad to worse. Frank told our employees that there was no money to pay them and begged them to stay on, hinting at big rewards when things picked up. Suppliers went unpaid and bills stacked up.

Even so, I somehow managed to hold on to a shred of hope that

I would see my money again—until I got his call notifying me of the eviction. When I got to the restaurant, Frank told me everything in the restaurant was going to be gone the next day, so I could take whatever I wanted. He also told me there would be no recovery of my investment.

I loaded up my car with cooking utensils, plants, and boxes of napkins and drove away. I kept those plants for years as my most valuable possessions. I kidded with my wife years later, saying, "Those are all that's left of my investment, honey, so that plant by the couch is worth about a thousand dollars...that one over in the corner is worth a thousand dollars...this pizza cutter is worth another thousand dollars..." The jokes helped ease my pain a bit, but just under the surface, the loss still stung.

For years I looked back at that time in my life with regret and shame. How could I have been so stupid to throw away all that money? But then I realized something that forever changed my perspective of that incident.

I realized that I was in a small, elite club of people in this world who dare to try. My goal was to own my own business, to be my own boss. The problem was that I had no idea how to go about it. So I tried something, got beaten up financially, learned a few things, and then tried again. This process is the Power of Failure. The mastery of this power is one of the principle differences between the successful and the mediocre.

Don't get me wrong. I don't like failing. No winner does. But people who are successful in their careers, relationships, and business ventures recognize failure for what it is: a stern tutor who raps your knuckles with a ruler until you learn your lesson and get it right.

Mediocre folks seek to avoid failure at all costs. They would rather do anything than suffer the heartache, embarrassment, and grief of falling on their face. They point to others' failure as proof of their wisdom in choosing not to venture. They make it their ambition to seek a life of safety. But as I mentioned earlier, there is no such thing as safety. The world is a dangerous place. If your goal is to be safe, you're chasing a mirage. Only when you abandon the idea of safety can you begin your growth journey.

Finding My Voice

People often ask me how I became a speaker. They ask me if I have always wanted to be a humorous speaker or comedian, and the answer is no. I wanted to be a musician.

I have loved music as long as I can remember, but when I heard rock 'n' roll for the first time, there was no turning back. I was around seven years old when I discovered a Saturday morning TV show featuring a group of young musicians singing their songs and having whacky adventures. Long before MTV and music videos, there were the Monkees, lip-syncing their songs and pretending to play instruments on network television. What could be more cool to a seven-year-old? I would have given anything to be Davy Jones, but I would have settled for being any of them.

When I was fourteen, I taught myself to play my mom's old ukulele. That convinced my parents to buy a beginner guitar for me that I had been begging for. I was already playing drums in the school band, and it wasn't long before I began jamming with other musicians and playing in garage bands.

When I graduated high school, I moved 100 miles from home under the pretense of going to college, but my real motive was to rejoin my high school friends and create a new rock band. When that band fizzled out, I decided that the solo singer-songwriter route was the path for me. I began to take my guitar and play my songs anywhere and everywhere I thought my talents might be needed and appreciated.

I can't tell you the number of homeless shelters, nursing homes, senior centers, youth groups, and fairs I've played. My objective was to live a life of purpose and value by using my talents and abilities to help others. After a few years of these events in the trenches, I found myself making a living by traveling all over the southeastern United States, visiting hundreds of churches as their musical guest.

I was recording a self-produced album in the early '90s when I noticed a growing fatigue in my voice. It wasn't long before my throat started feeling sore and my singing voice began to be raspy at times. As these symptoms worsened, I decided I needed to see a doctor and get some tests run. During one of the tests, a technician stuck a rod with a camera on the end of it down my throat as I made different sounds ("aahhh…eee…ooo…") while trying not to gag.

From my point of view, the tests proved pretty useless, other than eliminating all the things that were not wrong with me. The doctor said my vocal chords didn't have any nodes on them and only seemed red and irritated. Years later I would learn that acid reflux was burning my vocal chords and ruining my singing voice.

All the while, my singing career was heading from bad to disastrous. I needed to wrap up my album because I needed the tracks to send to churches that were considering hosting me. I had nothing to send out, so no bookings were coming in, and my finances were badly hemorrhaging.

This, of course, caused incredible pressure in my marriage. As my voice was failing and my career was in a tailspin, my wife and I regularly argued about money. As the process dragged on and on, the arguing became more regular and intense. My wife demanded to know what my plan was to fix our finances, and I didn't have a clue where to begin.

Amazingly, either due to my obstinacy or my denial, I was still performing. Not performing very well, mind you, but performing. I began doing fewer songs per set, leaning more on my jokes and stories between songs. For the most part, the crowds seemed to like the humor and still enjoyed my program.

By the mid-1990s, after years of dealing with my vocal problems, I gradually realized it was time to face reality and say goodbye to a lifelong dream. I would never again be able to sing professionally. But what should I do to make a living instead?

My choices were obvious. I could move on, find something else to do, and apply the lessons I had learned to future endeavors, or I could try to cling to the past in a fairy-tale world, believing that someday something would change and that my voice and music career would somehow magically reappear.

After much soul-searching, prayer, and consultation with people whose opinion I trusted, I chose to drop the music from my program and become a full-time comedian. That decision was one of the best

I've made in my life. After I made the switch from music to comedy, my career catapulted from a regional to a national level.

It turned out that comedians who did clean humor were in big demand back in the '90s. Blue, or off-color, humor might have been big in the clubs back then, but the corporate and church crowds didn't want or need club-type humor. They needed something that was funny but that wouldn't offend their most sensitive audience member. Consequently, I did quite well, and doors opened for me to do my act all over the country.

The point I'm making in this story is that when failure knocks on your door, when all seems lost and your dreams die right in front of your eyes, your story is not over. Regardless of what happens to you, regardless of how dark your situation seems, no matter how bad life has kicked you in the teeth, no matter how beaten up you are, you always have another move.

Before I lost my singing voice, I saw myself one-dimensionally— as a musician and nothing more. Before my voice deteriorated, I never realized that I am a multifaceted being. I never guessed that I could have a career as a comedian and speaker. The thought would never have occurred to me that I could run a business, manage a staff, or write columns and books.

In retrospect, I can see that the devastation of my former aspirations bought me my freedom. I couldn't see it at the time, but I had been a prisoner. I was locked into a cage built from fantasy and lack of vision. But that experience taught me that I'm bigger than I thought I was. I found that my voice is bigger than my ability to sing, and my song is stronger than rhythm and melody.

Some people would nod their heads and say, "Yes, Charles. When God closes a door, he opens a window," but I think that statement is way off the mark. I definitely felt God's comfort and leading during those times, but the truth is, the window was always open. I just didn't see it. I had the latent ability to be more, but until my dreams of being a musician crashed and burned, I was unaware of the other abilities I possessed. Failure made me look for the window. And then it made me bust out the wall and make another door to walk through.

If you are alert to possibilities and willing to make some tough decisions, you will often find that the opportunities on your new path will eclipse those of your old path. Why? Because you take the skills, lessons, and wisdom you have acquired and apply them to your new endeavors. Your story is never over while you are still drawing breath (and I believe it's not really even over then).

Conclusion

As you've read this chapter, I'm sure you've recalled a few times in your own life when failure has challenged you. Maybe you even see how it has pushed you farther along the path toward fulfilling your potential. Now, I want to ask you two questions to help you measure the way failure is presently affecting your life.

1. Are you failing enough? I know it sounds strange to ask that question, but remember, you are thinking of failure in a whole new way. You now see failure as a necessary step toward reaching your potential.

If you aren't failing at anything in life, you aren't challenging yourself. You aren't attempting to do anything beyond your present levels of skill and knowledge. On the other hand, if you are pushing yourself to do things you've never attempted, failure will often be a natural consequence.

So when you look at your life, how many blips of failure do you see on your radar? Is it dotted with ugly mistakes and errors you've made as you reached to be more than you are? Or does the radar screen show all clear? *All clear* sounds good if you're an air-traffic controller, but if you're monitoring growth in your life, *all clear* means nothing is going on. There are no accidents to report because there is no traffic. No traffic means no attempts. No attempts means no growth. No growth means no success.

2. Are you avoiding failure? Of course, nobody wants more failure in his or her life. Success is a lot more fun and much less painful. But if you're going to succeed, you cannot afford to shy away from risk simply because of the possibility of failure. By avoiding risk, you ensure your doom. Instead, you must continue to risk, to make the attempt, to dare to scale the mountain and take the next challenge of your journey.

Your Stern Tutor

Exercise your imagination with me for a moment. Imagine you're sitting on a piano bench, practicing your scales on an old upright piano. Beside you sits an old Russian piano master who intently watches your exercises. He holds a small ruler in his hand, and when you play the wrong note, he deftly slaps your knuckles with a ruler. It hurts every time he hits you, and you hate it every time it happens. You intently dislike the old man and vow that he will have less of an opportunity to rap your knuckles. You will practice and make sure you rob him of the satisfaction of correcting you.

The name of the old teacher is Failure. You don't have to like him. You don't have to approve of his methods. You didn't hire him and you can't fire him. You only need to be aware of his presence and make sure you learn from him.

The most important revelation about Failure is that he isn't your enemy. He is your lifelong companion and friend. His purpose is to make you grow. To make you better. Throwing a tantrum or pouting won't make him relent in his mission to teach you. There are no short-cuts to get around him. The only way forward is through him.

Sure, you can get up from the bench and go play. You can ignore his instruction, but tomorrow you will be sitting beside him again, getting your knuckles rapped. Learn his lessons or experience pain.

Imagine for a moment that failure isn't your final destination. Imagine that it is just a chapter in the amazing story of your life. Imagine that one day you will look back on your present trials and wonder what you thought was so difficult about this stage in your development. Imagine yourself graduating to more difficult pieces of music with new challenges, new responsibilities, and new rewards.

POWER OF FAILURE APPLICATION QUESTIONS—
Packing Your Emergency Roadside Repair Kit

1. At what project or relationship have you utterly failed? What is your attitude about that failure?

2. Do you condemn yourself for blowing it, or do you congratulate yourself for having the courage to try?

3. What lessons did you learn from your failure that will help keep you from repeating that same mistake in the future? Have you taken steps to implement those lessons?

4. How has the way you have viewed your failures prevented you from implementing the Power of Action?

GROUP DISCUSSION QUESTIONS

1. What past failures have you allowed to define you?

2. How can the perspective of having experienced a failure help you in future endeavors?

3. Give an example of how you have learned from a specific failure in your life and how that will help you move forward.

6

The Power of
CHARACTER

I'm starting to lose track of all the teen idols we've had in this country. I think one of the reasons is that after a while, they all look so much alike. The faces change, but their stories pretty much are identical.

A young actor or singer blasts onto the national stage, and everyone under the age of 16 is talking about him. His picture graces the cover of scores of magazines. You can't turn on the radio without hearing his songs. He frequently makes television appearances and might even have a television show of his own. His concerts are always sold out and are packed with thousands of screaming girls.

But then a few years pass. His audience grows up, grows tired of him, and moves on. His records don't sell as well, and his TV show is cancelled. You can still see him on magazine covers, but they're different magazines, and he's there for a different reason. Now we find out that our star is quite the party boy. The paparazzi catch him coming out of a club in the wee hours of the morning looking disheveled and bleary eyed. We see the mug shot from his first arrest. We see him entering rehab.

And then we see all of these pictures again. And again. Our young star just can't seem to get over the fact that he's not a star anymore, and he spends a lifetime trying to recapture the attention and glory he fed on during the formative years of his life.

There was one teen idol, however, who chose a different path. It was impossible to go anywhere without seeing his picture, including my own house. My sister adored him and wallpapered her room with his posters. His songs, such as "Julie, Do Ya Love Me?" and "Easy Come, Easy Go," floated through the rooms of my home. And when he made guest appearances on TV shows—*The Partridge Family*, *The Monkees*, *American Bandstand*, and *The Sonny & Cher Comedy Hour*—my sister's excitement level rocketed. Eventually he starred in a TV show called *Here Come the Brides*, which my sister also watched faithfully.

Bobby Sherman was one of the biggest stars of the early seventies. But then, as always happens, his star burned less and less brilliantly until he faded from public eye.

But Bobby's real success story began after his stardom. Instead of crashing and burning in a life of excess, indulgence, and self-pity, he found new purpose in becoming an emergency medical technician. Although he would continue to make the occasional appearance on a television show over the years, his real job became investing his life and offering his time and skills to help others in his community. Through the years, he has become known the world over as a person of substance and character. He doesn't make any claim to be perfect, but he's one of those rare individuals who validated the trust and admiration of the many fans who loved him in the late '60s and early '70s.

The Frame of Your Success Vehicle

How far do you plan to travel on your success journey? Is your success vehicle built to take you all the way? Is its frame strong enough to withstand the rigors of the journey? How much pressure and punishment will your character frame withstand?

And will it support not only you but also all those who ride with you on your trip? People rarely consider that last question, but when your character breaks down, all those around you suffer as well. Your family, coworkers, and friends all are affected when your character malfunctions.

But what does being a person of character even mean? Does it really even matter whether you have character?

The importance of character used to be a given. Years ago, nobody would have seriously argued that people's character wasn't a crucial element of their involvement in an organization. But things have changed. Sometime over the past few decades, people started asking, what does it really matter if a person has character as long as he can perform his job adequately?

As I've studied the subject, I've found character to be a critical element of success that cannot and must not be overlooked. Over the years, people have booked me to speak to their groups about character many times, not so much because I'm the expert on all things character, but because character is an important subject that people care a great deal about. Many people still realize that character does indeed count, and they want the people in their organizations to value its importance.

Will the Qualified Expert Please Step Forward?

After speaking and writing about the subject for many years, I've identified two problems with character presentations, whether oral or written.

The first problem I've already alluded to, and that is that if someone is speaking to you about character, the inference is that his life represents the epitome of character. He has it all together, and therefore, he's the right person to speak to you on the subject. I'm uncomfortable with that notion because no one has it all together in the character department. No author, preacher, or motivational speaker has perfect character, and if you find one who tells you that he does…well, consider that a major character flaw.

No one's character is anywhere near perfect, myself included. But having conceded that point, can't we agree that even though we are all flawed creatures, there are things about character we can still learn together?

The second problem with character presentations is that speakers and authors tend to spank their audiences. When you boil away all the excess verbiage, the gist of the message usually comes down to telling people that what they're doing isn't cutting it, so they need to try harder. The message is, what you are and who you are aren't good enough, so you need to do better—or else! (Cue scary music.) People come away from hearing this type of message feeling beaten up rather than inspired and empowered to reach their potential.

My goal in all of my character presentations is not to moralize about the subject but to look at it from a perspective of success versus failure. How is one's life affected if one makes choices that are perceived as evidence of a good character? How about when the reverse is true? What happens to a person who either doesn't value character or who doesn't consider the subject at all?

My objective is to show that character is vital to your success. I want you to see how developing and focusing on your character will not only make you the person you desire to be but also to propel you forward in your career and personal relationships.

Character Counts

I got my very first "cease and desist" letter from the attorney of a talent agency in California. The letter was written in stern, threatening language, warning that if I did not stop using trademarked phrases on my website, the agency would bring action against me.

Just as these letters are meant to do, this one scared me. Not the type of scared you get by driving in a blizzard, but scared nonetheless. And to be perfectly honest, it also rankled me a bit. I didn't like being threatened, and part of me wanted to fight back. I had heard a long time ago that when an attorney is threatening you, you don't contact him yourself, you answer back with an attorney of your own. So I called an attorney and spoke to him about the situation. He suggested that we could do this or that, and then we got off the phone.

After we hung up, I thought and prayed about the situation for a while. The more I thought about it, the more I didn't like the multiple-choice options being presented on my exam. I wondered if there might be another path I might take. I also wondered exactly what wording on my website had caused this aggression. How was I being perceived by the owner of the agency? What was he under the impression that I was trying to do?

I had never spoken with the owner of this agency before, although I had tried numerous times. He had a successful agency representing clean comedy acts, so I thought I would be a good candidate for its roster. Every time I called him to introduce myself though, his receptionist intercepted my call and gave me the runaround. "Just send us your information packet and we'll take a look at it." She told me the agency received seven to ten packets a week, so she couldn't even promise that my packet would get reviewed. From time to time I tried calling them, but I never could get any further than the receptionist.

But now, I figured that if their attorney had sent me a letter…well, they had to know who I was, right? If their attorney had written me, the owner had probably given him my name and had at least heard of me and knew who I was. True, he probably considered me at best a pest and at worst an enemy, but I couldn't help wondering what might happen if I called and asked to speak to the owner now.

I picked up the phone, dialed the agency's number, and asked for the owner of the company. The receptionist took my name, and shortly afterward, I heard the voice of the owner, whom I had been trying to reach for the past three or four years. At first he was understandably a bit defensive, but when he saw that I wasn't there to fight but to cooperate and help, he loosened up and became quite friendly.

I told him it wasn't my intention to steal any apples out of his orchard. I assured him I wasn't trying to get away with anything, and I apologized for the mistake. Then I did something that really caught him off guard. I said, "Are you online right now?"

"Uh, yeah," he answered, sounding a little wary of where I might be headed.

"Would you mind pulling up my website right now and telling me where I'm messing up?"

"Um…sure, I guess I could do that," he answered. We spent the next few minutes reviewing the language of my website. After a couple of minutes, I noticed that some of the things that initially bugged him didn't bother him so much anymore.

After we came to an understanding about my website's language, I broached the subject of his agency representing me. He told me to send my packet and he would be happy to personally review it.

I mailed my packet, and shortly afterward, I was listed on the roster for his agency. Over the next several years, I received many bookings through that agency. Years later, the owner of the agency told me he had been impressed with my character that first day we spoke, and one of the reasons he wanted to work with me was because of our initial encounter.

It's not my intention to paint myself as the epitome of character. I'm not saying I didn't have an ulterior motive in calling him. But I was sincere when I spoke to him and told him I wasn't trying to rip him off. I really didn't mean to do anything wrong, and I wanted to straighten the whole thing out if we could.

But I think the most important lesson this story has to offer is that people are always watching your character. They are paying attention to your actions and measuring your character, even when you are not aware of it. It never crossed my mind that the agency owner was looking at my character or that character might be an important measuring stick to him. But it was important to me that I treated him right, and he sensed that value and responded accordingly.

I have worked with his company plenty of times over the years since then, and it has put thousands of dollars in my pocket. None of that would have happened if the agency owner had continued in his belief that I was trying to steal his brand. The fact that I came forward and tried to fix the problem convinced him that I was someone with whom he wanted to work.

How often do people measure our character without our even knowing it? How many times do we either get or miss the deal because the buyer is evaluating what he sees? How many times do people get rejected in relationships because the prospective partners find their character lacking?

We might not like that we're being evaluated, or we might not agree with the standard by which we are being measured. But one thing is for certain—the world is watching us and making decisions that affect our future based on our character.

What I Mean When I Say *Character*

If someone asked you to define character, what would you say? The word *character* is a bit like the word *success*. Most people use the word regularly but rarely stop to consider its meaning or its application in their own lives. Ask people what they think character is, and chances are, you'll get as many answers as the number of people you ask.

I believe your character is the silent answer to the question, what kind of person are you? It is the sum of who you are. It is your substance. It is the reflection and residue of your actions.

Character and Reputation

Your character extends far beyond your reputation. It goes further than what other people think of you. You may have a poor reputation in your community, but that doesn't necessarily mean you have poor character. As a matter of fact, it might mean the opposite.

If character demands that you dare to stand up for what is right and go against status quo, you may very well be ostracized by your community. The people in your community may not share your standards of morality. They may follow a different code of behavior that causes them to think poorly of you. Sometimes having character means being misunderstood, unpopular, and scorned.

A person of character may have a good reputation. A person with a good reputation may have good character. But true character remains steady in the face of opposition, even at the cost of reputation. It doesn't give thought to appearance, nor does it bow to the pressures of societal influence. Despite the changing fads of perceived morality and the winds of popular consent, some things are a constant in the universe. I like to think that one of those things is character.

What Does Character Look Like?

What traits make up the essential components of character? Well, that answer also depends on whom you ask. Some companies have a list of character traits that their leaders feel are valuable. Many school districts post similar lists so their students will understand the behavior expected of them. Fraternal organizations often publish character traits in their organizational literature.

The traits vary from group to group, depending on the value each group places on those particular traits. No one list of character traits is definitive, but even so, most lists generally contain many of the same traits. The following list isn't intended to be an exhaustive compilation of all the traits of character, but of some of the most popular traits that most people associate with the subject.

Persistence

> Left–left–right–right–left
> Right–right–left–left–right
> Left–left–right–right–left
> Right–right–left–left–right
> Repeat

Over and over and over again. And then do it about a zillion more times.

It's called a five-stroke drum roll and is one of the very first drum rudiments I learned. I had only been playing drums for about a week when our band director announced a tryout, which is a competition among kids playing the same instrument to see who gets to play the better, more complicated parts, who gets to play any solos, and who has the prestige of being named first chair.

A piece of music, a scale, or in my case, a drum rudiment is selected by the band director, and then several days are spent letting each kid play his assigned piece of music while the band director grades the performances and everyone else listens.

I started playing drums about six or eight weeks into the second year of junior high band. I had come into the game later than everyone else and had only been playing drums for about a week, so I asked the band director if I would be required to also try out. He told me he saw no reason why not. I could think of about a hundred reasons why not—all of them my classmates, laughing at me while I made an idiot of myself. I was terrified. I was already pretty unpopular and wasn't looking to get more attention, which would no doubt translate into humiliation.

So I was motivated to practice, and practice I did. But no matter how much work I put into it, I didn't seem to be getting any better. The night before tryouts, I stood in front of my drum in my bedroom and had a temper tantrum. My mom came to my room to find out what the problem was, and with tears in my eyes, I told her I wasn't any good playing drums and I was going to humiliate myself the next day.

My mom told me that I had begged to play drums and that the band director seemed to think I could do it, so I could stand there and cry, or I could practice and do the best I could.

Left–left–right–right–left
Right–right–left–left–right
Repeat

The next day I tried out and made second chair. Two weeks later, I challenged the girl ahead of me and won first chair. I held it for the rest of the year.

I didn't realize at the time that I was learning something far more important than drum rudiments. I was learning to persist under pressure. Persistence is the act of putting one foot in front of the other when you least feel like it. It is the voice that commands you to keep moving forward when everything inside screams at you to quit.

If you will develop the habit of persistence, that one trait will place you miles ahead of your competition simply because the great majority of people are in the habit of giving up when things get too tough.

Your first step in developing persistence is to decide whether an action or activity is something you really want. In junior high school, I wanted more than anything to play drums. I ate, walked, talked, slept, and thought about drums all the time. When things got hard, my mom reminded me of the way I felt about drumming when there wasn't any pressure, and I found the will to continue.

You need to decide what you think about an activity or relationship before the hard times come. Don't wait until you're in a pressure situation to decide whether you want to be there. Don't wait until you're getting shot at to decide whether you want to be in the army. When you're under fire, that is the time to fight and advance.

After you've determined that an activity or relationship is something you want, commit to it and move forward. It sounds easy, but it's not. If it were, everybody would be happily married, rich, and successful. But the fact is, most people quit too soon.

Which sort of person are you? Do you throw up your hands when things get tough, or do you trudge through the ugly stuff to get where you want to be? Do you keep dialing the phone even when nobody wants to buy from you, or do you give yourself an excuse to quit? Do you take marriage classes and learn communication skills, or do you bail at the first sign of trouble?

You will need to learn to press on, march forward, and climb upward if you are going to see the other side of the mountain. That's why you see most people hanging out in the valley. There is no challenge there. But neither is there any discovery.

Courage

In *Unbroken,* author Laura Hillenbrand tells the amazing story of World War II hero Louis Zamperini. Before the war, Louis had been a world-class runner representing the United States in the 1936 Olympics. As happened to so many others of his generation, his dreams were interrupted with the onset of World War II. Louis joined the US Air Corps, becoming a bombardier and serving in the South Pacific.

During a reconnaissance mission in May 1943, his plane and crew crashed into the Pacific Ocean. Louis survived the crash and drifted for 47 days in a small, ill-equipped life raft, battling constant hunger, thirst, and shark attacks. Louis drifted in his small craft some 2000 miles into Japanese waters before being rescued by the Japanese. His rescue replaced one nightmare with another as he was transferred to a Japanese prison camp, where he endured torture, beatings, and starvation.

Louis Zamperini is an American hero who suffered unimaginable hardship and lived to found and run a camp for troubled boys. If anyone makes a movie version of Louis's life, I plan to be one of the first people in line.

That kind of courage is exciting and inspirational to hear and read about, but courage doesn't always look like something you would see in a movie.

Not long ago, a family friend was mowing his lawn when he suffered a heart attack and died, leaving three daughters and a pregnant wife. My wife and I watched in respectful amazement as the young widow grieved the loss of her husband while mothering her children and giving birth to their fourth child. She displayed a grace, dignity, and courage that we have rarely seen.

Sometimes courage is quiet.

Most of the time courage is not a brash defiance or a loud, brazen gesture. Many times it's a single mom working two jobs to put food on the table. Or it's a policeman going to work every day, not knowing if it will be his last. Or it's a teacher battling budget cuts and defiant kids. Or it's an ER staff fighting to save an accident victim's life.

Are heroes fearless? No. Courage isn't the absence of fear, but the doing of one's duty in the face of fear. It's overcoming despair and employing the Power of Action to do what needs to be done. It's moving forward to care for others when your knees are weak and your heart is clutched in fear.

Where would we all be without the courageous? How many marriages would last? How many businesses would thrive? How many children would be raised?

I believe everyone has it within their heart to be a hero. Everyone has the ability to be courageous. Courage is a choice.

Where does your courage stand? When it is your time to offer yourself, what will you do? Courage doesn't have to look pretty. It doesn't have to have the right words. It just has to show up and stand.

Integrity

In 2004 I found a foreclosure property that I really liked. The house had been vacant for at least a couple of years and was in serious need of renovation. But the house had great potential and was priced to sell, so I thought it would be a great idea to buy it and fix it up myself. I was about half right.

I bought the home and then worked on it for about a month before

I realized that I don't like remodeling houses. I would much rather have a microphone in my hand than a hammer. So I began contracting out some of the work. That's when I got in touch with Bernie.

I first met Bernie a few years earlier when he worked as a car salesman. He was a friend of a friend, so we occasionally bumped into each another socially. We had lost touch with each other over the years but reconnected after I heard that Bernie had set up shop as a handyman, doing home remodeling. I thought Bernie might be a good solution to my contracting dilemma. He claimed to be able to do several of the repairs needed, and since we had known each other on and off over the years, we had an easy rapport. But I soon learned that knowing someone socially and paying him to work for you are two different things.

I had problems with Bernie right from the beginning. He rarely showed up when he said he was going to, if he showed up at all. Then he would arrive on the job site a few days later as if nothing had happened. It was all a big misunderstanding, he told me. Were we going to meet on Tuesday? I thought it was Thursday. The excuses never ended.

When I decided that Bernie and I needed to go separate ways, I asked him for my bill and received my final surprise. Bernie had padded the bill with charges for several trips he had taken to the hardware store to pick up supplies. The funny thing was, it wasn't the extra charges themselves that bothered me. This is America. If Bernie wants to charge for trips to the store, he has that right. What bothered me is that he was running a silent meter and never bothered to tell me. After all the other times he had broken his word to me, I looked at these charges very suspiciously.

I disputed the charges, and we worked out a compromise, but that was the last time I ever did business with Bernie. I have rental property and still have need of folks who know which end of a hammer to hold, but I'll never use Bernie again. Not because I'm mad at Bernie. I have no emotion attached to my decision not to use his services at all. It's just that I've learned that I can't trust him to keep his word, so I'm going to save myself the time and trouble of dealing with him and choose someone else to help me.

Your word is who you are. If you commit to it, you have to follow through. Most people understand when something goes awry once or twice, but when you break your word habitually, it speaks volumes about your character.

Keeping your word means something. Our society is built on our trust in one another. Our world crumbles into chaos if we don't keep our word, if we default on our loans, if our marriage vows mean nothing, if we don't raise our children, if we don't show up for work.

Integrity is one of the main beams of your character frame. How strong is yours? Do people know you as a person of integrity, a person they can count on to follow through and keep your word? Do you say what you do and do what you say? How strong would your friends, relatives, and coworkers say your integrity is?

Discipline

I broached the subject of discipline when I talked about learning to play the drums. Anyone who has learned to play an instrument or paint or play a sport knows that type of discipline—playing a phrase over and over until you get it right, running a play until it is seamless, practicing a brush stroke until you can do it in your sleep.

I wish every child could have the opportunity of learning to play an instrument or a sport. Something essential is built into your character from the practice of making yourself do something over and over again until you have it right. You are learning to master yourself, to make yourself do something you don't want to do in order to get to where you want to be. No wonder expert musicians and painters are called masters.

There are masters in this world who use discipline to move themselves and their organizations, families, and causes forward. And then there are the mastered, those who scorn discipline because it isn't enjoyable. The mastered avoid difficulty today only to have it return to them tomorrow with compound interest due.

Which are you, the master or the mastered? Do you see discipline as a ticket to success or a restraint keeping you from doing what you want? As you think about that question, let's take a moment to define a couple areas of discipline that affect our everyday lives.

The discipline of work. What is your work ethic? What kind of worker would those around you say you are? Do you continue to work when you don't feel like it, or do you habitually allow yourself to quit when you encounter obstacles like fatigue, injury, or heartache? A good work ethic says…

- If a job is worth doing, it's worth doing well.

- I am responsible for making it happen.

- I finish what I start, and I will complete this project on time.

- If I'm on time for work, I'm actually five minutes late. I should be sitting in my chair with my fingers on the keyboard when it's time to be at work.

- I am the first to arrive and the last to leave.

A poor work ethic says…

- Everything will probably work out all right without me doing anything.

- It's not my problem.

- Someone else will take care of it.

- Being on time to work means driving up to the building on time.

- I am at work only until the moment I'm allowed to leave.

The discipline of self-control. Are you someone who seeks immediate gratification, or do you make yourself wait a bit? Do you tell yourself you have to have everything now, or do you wait for a later reward? When you want something, do you reach for the credit card, or do you set aside money over time to buy it? Self-control says…

- I will wait to buy it until I can afford it.

- I will wait for a commitment before giving myself away in a relationship.

- I will treat my body well today so that I can count on it tomorrow.

- I will build my financial house brick by brick.

- I will reserve my opinion until I know it will do good and not harm.

> **HERE'S A THOUGHT...**
>
> Discipline is the buy-in of your success. If you don't believe in discipline, you are not invested in creating your own success.

Lack of self-control says...

- I deserve to have everything now.

- It makes me feel good, so I will do it.

- I will eat, drink, and ingest any substance I want.

- I want to get rich quickly.

- I always say what's on my mind regardless of the consequences.

Giving

One day when I attended the University of Southern Mississippi, I bumped into my friend Lynn on campus, and I asked how her she was doing. She told me she was struggling financially at the moment and wasn't even sure she had enough food to make it through the end of the week. I thought for a moment, reached in my wallet, and handed her my last ten-dollar bill. I didn't tell Lynn that it was all the money I had left until payday three days from then. I figured that if push came to shove, I could just not eat for a few days. I prayed and asked God to meet my needs and then sat back to watch what would happen.

The next day at work, my boss at the retail store where I was employed announced a surprise one-day sales contest with a $20 prize. All day long it seemed as though I was tripping over people who wanted to buy clothes from me. At the end of the day I found out I won the contest and picked up my $20.

I've had people tell me that that kind of thing is just coincidence, but I've had it happen to me far too many times to dismiss it as chance. I believe I was operating within a universal principle as solid as the law of gravity. The principle goes by many names. Some people call it the law of reciprocity. Some people call it the law of sowing and reaping. Some people just say, "What goes around, comes around." But all of these phrases mean the same thing: The things you do have a way of finding their way back to you. If you plant your resources, time, and talents in others' lives, you'll find that those seeds will bloom and produce a crop again in your own life.

In 1994, due to the problems I was having with my voice that I mentioned in chapter 5, my wife and I netted a combined income that was well below poverty level. Those were thin times financially for us. We almost never ate out. We didn't buy new clothes, furniture, or cars. We ate a lot of rice and homemade soup.

But the really interesting part about that time in our lives was getting to experience firsthand the law of sowing and reaping. During that time we continued to financially support our church and were even able to sponsor a little girl in Haiti for a year. We were involved in numerous other giving projects as well.

Even with all our penny-pinching that year, it's hard to figure out how we made it. We not only survived but also didn't go into debt at all that year. Financial responsibility was an important part of our survival, but the law of reciprocity was also working for us. To people who have never operated with this principle, it sounds like a lot of superstitious hooey, but to those who have experienced it, it's a fact of life.

I could fill a book with all the times I've seen this principle in operation. But the main point I want to communicate about the importance of making giving a part of your character has nothing to do with the excitement of seeing what you've planted come back to you.

In fact, seeing this principle come to life is only a secondary benefit of giving. The real adventure is being the miracle in someone else's life. I can't tell you how cool it is to be the answer to someone's prayer, especially if your deed is done anonymously. I believe in God and prayer and the spiritual world, but when a material miracle happens, it is because someone's heart was touched and he was moved to give of his own possessions.

I don't have an agenda in talking to you about the importance of giving. I'm not trying to get into your pocket. I'm not selling anything or looking for you to contribute to my cause. I'm reporting my findings from a lifetime of studying the subject. Do what you want, but my advice is to employ the Power of Action and find a way to give to your community. The most successful people always do.

Are there other character traits? Sure…how much time do you have? We could talk all day long about traits like these:

- humility—being able and willing to admit wrongdoing, apologize, and make restitution
- loyalty—remaining true to your allegiances and standing firm in your commitments
- selflessness—putting other people's needs and desires ahead of your own
- kindness—expressing consideration and helpfulness to others

The choice of which character traits you admire and acquire is up to you, but understand that they are all applicable in every area of your life.

Good Character Gone Bad—How Did That Happen?

"What could have happened to my boy?" Karen asked.

On a flight from Denver to Atlanta, Karen and I sat next to each other and struck up a conversation. Eventually, we made our way around to the subject of families, and Karen confided that she was having trouble with her 19-year-old son, Craig.

She had raised Craig by herself since her husband had passed away when Craig was only eight years old. When Craig started having trouble in school, she changed jobs so she could be at home more often. She also sent Craig to a private Christian school that supported her values. Both of the changes seemed to help her son immensely, but now that he had graduated high school, she had begun to notice some disturbing traits. Craig was staying out until the wee hours of the morning, and she suspected that when he was home, he just sat around the house smoking dope. Craig had a part-time job and went to college. He even regularly attended church, but all those things did little to curtail his partying ways.

Now Karen worried about him much of the time. She also wondered what had happened to Craig. He had been heading in a positive direction, and then seemingly out of nowhere, Craig had veered off the straight and narrow. He had been one person one day, and then overnight he turned into someone else. Where had this other person come from? Which person represented the real Craig?

What We're Up Against

A serious man in a dark laboratory contemplates a small vial of liquid briefly before upending the contents into his mouth. Almost immediately after swallowing the concoction, his face contorts in spasms of unthinkable pain. Slowly, his countenance begins to contort, transforming by degree into a grotesque mask of evil incarnate. Dr. Jekyll has once again transformed into his alter ego, the heinous Mr. Hyde.

I've seen depictions of this transformation all my life. Dozens of movies and television shows have reimagined this famous scene, sometimes adding a new element or two but always adhering to the formula of a normal man turning into a horrific monster.

It is a mystery to me, though, how *The Strange Case of Dr. Jekyll and Mr. Hyde* ever got its reputation as a horror story. Mr. Hyde is often mentioned in the same breath as Dracula, Frankenstein, and the Wolf Man, but when you read Robert Louis Stevenson's original story, it is anything but a typical horror story.

His story tells of Henry Jekyll, a brilliant scientist who discovers that man's soul is divided into two parts, good and evil. He invents two potions, the first of which turns him into the evil part of himself (Edward Hyde), allowing him to fully explore the darker side of his nature. The second potion is an antidote to the effects of the first potion, which turns him back into the kind and benevolent Dr. Jekyll.

As Dr. Jekyll continues to indulge his darker inclinations through the person of Mr. Hyde, he makes the alarming discovery that the transformation back to the good part of himself is becoming increasingly difficult. Additionally, he begins involuntarily turning into Mr. Hyde, even when he hasn't taken the potion to do so. Eventually, his potion to return himself to Dr. Jekyll again loses its effectiveness, and the person of Dr. Jekyll is lost within the darkness that is Mr. Hyde.

The true horror of the story is not the thought of encountering a fiend like Mr. Hyde on the street, but the idea of being overtaken and dominated by the Mr. Hyde that lies within us. The lesson of the story is that if you feed and indulge your dark nature, it will one day consume and control you.

Moral Entropy

In answer to Karen's question about her son's transformation, the hard truth is that nothing needs to happen for people to slide because we all live on a hill. We are all subject to moral entropy.

Entropy is the second law of thermodynamics, which basically states that everything in the universe is going from a state of order to disorder. Rocks break down and turn into dirt. Stars eventually burn out. Laundry doesn't fold itself and put itself away. Without intervention, order dissolves into chaos.

Our nature is subject to a type of entropy as well. We all have a Mr. Hyde lurking beneath the surface. We all have a proclivity to slide down the hill. And to roll down the character hill requires no effort. Iron doesn't have to try to rust, and you don't have to try to have corroded character. It happens naturally if you don't make an effort to stop it.

Three Things You Should Know About Your Evil Twin

1. People never wake up and decide they're going to be evil. Bad character always arrives in small parcels, one compromise at a time. Criminals aren't born; they're made. All of us are born with the inclination and capability to do wrong, but the question is, will we climb up the character hill or slide down it?

2. Evil is best defined as selfishness unrestrained. Evil rarely ever

looks scary. Most evil you encounter doesn't have glowing eyes and isn't surrounded by a mist. Most evil looks casual and harmless. It looks like someone offering an elderly person an investment opportunity. It looks like a stranger offering a child a ride home. It looks like money being collected for a national tragedy (with no accountability for how the money will be spent). It looks like governments offering reform and benefits (in exchange for freedoms). It looks like a husband leaving his wife and kids because he's "fallen out of love" and has found someone else "who appreciates him for who he is."

3. People never think of themselves as the bad guy. They never think of themselves as evil. You may argue that you've known people who have bragged about how "bad" they were, but the truth is, they most likely pictured themselves not as evil, but as cool. Most people can vividly remember when their heart was first broken, or when something was stolen from them, or when they were mistreated at work. But they have a difficult time recalling the people whose hearts they've broken, the things they've "appropriated," or the times they mistreated their employer.

Community Transference

The second reason Karen's son may have strayed has to do with what I call community transference. Community transference is the switch from one community, along with all its corresponding values and mores, to another community and its alternative values.

Ask almost anyone you meet about the origin of his values, and he will tell you he is the author of his own life philosophy. Most people believe they have the values they do simply because of who they are or because those values are right and therefore they accepted them. But the truth is that most of the time, we choose a community and adapt to that community's values. The values of a collective form a community. Green Bay Packer fans are a community because of their passionate support for their team. Church people are a community because of their united faith. Some businesses have created a strong sense of community built on their corporate identity.

You can hang out with people in any of these communities, but if you don't share a group's values, remaining in that group will become very uncomfortable for you. If you break from the standard of behavior, you will generally find yourself no longer welcome in that community.

It is far easier to adopt the standards of those around you than to go against the flow, so the great majority of people in the world do just that. That's great news when a community seeks to help individuals climb the character hill. The recovering alcoholic can find support to sustain his resolve in an AA group or a church. A chamber of commerce can help young entrepreneurs learn about business. A grief recovery group can offer encouragement to the bereaved.

But the reverse is also true. It is said that bad company corrupts good morals, and those words could not be truer.

A Tale of Community Transference

Alton and Carol both worked for the phone company right out of college. He was a happy-go-lucky outside salesman, and she was an introverted computer programmer. It wasn't love at first sight, but after flirting with each other for a couple of weeks, Alton asked for her phone number, and they talked for four hours the first time he called. They dated for two years and got engaged on the second anniversary of their first date. Not quite a year later, they were married and busy setting up their new household.

They didn't have kids right away like some folks do, thinking it might be better to get to know each other for a while first. They traveled together, volunteered in their church, and bought a home. Just before their fifth anniversary, their first daughter, Kaley, was born, and then three years after that they were blessed with a son, Michael.

Alton changed jobs within the company several times, always working his way up the pay scale. He and his team were on the road at least two weeks out of every month, most of the time traveling out of state, sometimes even out of the country. Carol was busy homeschooling their two children, and though she was often harried and tired, she was otherwise happy with the course of their marriage.

There are only so many hours in a day you can spend in front of clients, and after-work time can hang heavy in your hands when you're on the road away from your family. For the first few months, Alton would hang out in his hotel room, working on contracts and returning e-mails, but that routine got old quickly.

He was in a Seattle hotel room around seven thirty on a Wednesday night when he heard a knock on his door. He found his whole team from work in the hotel hallway. They were going out sightseeing together and invited him. Saying no was not an option, so he grabbed his jacket and locked the hotel door behind him.

Several hours later, he was safely back in his room, no worse for the excursion. They had hit a few bars, had a few drinks, and had a few laughs, but nobody really overdid it, and he was able to get to know his team members a little better. It turned out that he had quite a bit in common with several of them.

Ricky Hammond and he had gone to the same college but had graduated in different years. They had a great time recounting the exploits of their alma mater's football team. He spoke briefly with Gerard Culpepper, who seemed to be just as into Madden NFL as he was, and they agreed to hit the virtual gridiron together soon. Most of his time, though, was spent with Ramona Tyler, who had a great sense of humor and absolutely lived for sports.

It was only natural that he and Ramona spent more time with each other over the next several months. He began to think of her as the kid sister he never had and felt protective of her when she was around other guys in a bar.

Their first kiss wasn't even on the lips, just a quick peck on the cheek at the hotel room door that no passerby would even give a second thought. A few nights later…well, the next one went far beyond an innocent kiss. That one wound up in bed. The next day they both swore that it was a one-time incident and that they would never stray into those waters again.

Two months later Alton found himself traveling to see Ramona at her home, two states away, inventing "business trips" to explain his multiple absences to his wife.

It seemed that not a day went by that he and Carol didn't fight now. Being around her led to a contentious, stress-filled life that he would much rather avoid. She constantly nagged him about being away from his home, his children, his responsibilities. When he was home, he couldn't wait until the next time he went out of town. When he was out of town, he couldn't bear to think of going home.

Carol found the pictures on Alton's laptop one night when Alton had run to the store. In one shot, Ramona was posing provocatively on a hotel bed. The next shot was of Alton—same room, same bed, same bedspread, same radio alarm clock. In another shot, he and Ramona lay together at arm's length, smiling into the camera.

Tears streamed down her face as she frantically packed her belongings and left the house with her children forever. Alton came home to find his laptop open and the pictures of him and Ramona mocking him.

Whatever happened to Alton? He never set out to leave his family. If you had told him five years earlier that he would be having an affair, he would have laughed at you. How does a person go from here to there without even intending to?

In Alton's case, the answer is simple. He changed his primary community from a family-based, church-oriented community to a dating, partying community. It doesn't take a rocket scientist to figure out that if you're away from your family consistently for two years, hanging out in bars with your single friends, your values are likely to change to reflect those of your new community.

Is it fair to say that Alton had no blame for his situation, and it was all the fault of his new friends and work circumstances? No, Alton had his Mr. Hyde to contend with too. Some people might say that Alton could have been stronger and not associated with people who would lead him astray, and that's true. But that type of strength—the kind that can stand alone, isolated from support, companionship, and comfort—is rare. We humans are made for community and rely on it. And since that community often underscores, defines, and reveals our character, it is vital to choose that community wisely.

If you're trying to have a successful family but you're hanging out with partying single folks, you might be single yourself before long. If you are trying to overcome a poverty mentality but the people in your core group are reinforcing consumer spending and keeping up with the Joneses, you could easily be dragged back down the character hill. If you are trying to prosper your business but you are attending meetings with people who are convinced that growth in this economy is impossible, you will most likely succumb to that way of thinking.

If the values of your community are corrosive, you should wear thick pants because my guess is that you'll be sliding down the character hill soon. If, however, the values of your community are uplifting, life-giving, and sustaining, then you have found a nurturing environment in which to grow.

Taking a Turn for the Better

What do Alcoholics Anonymous, Weight Watchers, and churches all have in common? All of them are communities of people who share similar values. Being a consistent member of one of these organizations means having to answer for your actions. Sure, they promote differing creeds, purposes, and methods, but the strength of these various creeds is enforced by the community that represents them.

You might be able to quit drinking by yourself without any help. But you're a lot more likely to succeed if you're a member of a community that supports that value. Of course you can lose weight without joining a weight-loss group. But if you're trying to drop some pounds, you would be wise to surround yourself with people who have adopted your philosophy about overeating.

The Other Side of the Community Transference Coin

One of the most delightful parts of my job is getting to connect with people after my presentations. After people hear me tell my tales and jokes, they feel as if they know me and can open up and tell their stories as well.

Not long ago, after I told my "Burning Bush" story, a gentleman named Carson approached me at the back of the room and told me he really related to that story. He told me that he too had been an alcoholic but had given it up almost 20 years ago. I asked Carson how he did it, and he said that prayer had been a huge part of his change. He had entered a rehab program and had been on his knees during the first two weeks of treatment, crying out to God for help. After his treatment program was over, he found a community of people who not only supported his life change but also stood by him and sought him out if he showed signs of weakening in his resolve.

Carson's story isn't unique. People come up to me all the time after hearing my "Burning Bush" story and tell me similar accounts. I can't tell you how many times I've heard the same story with the names and places changed. I've observed that in order for change to occur, two things have to happen. First, Mr. Hyde has to be dealt with. A real decision has to be made to turn around and climb back up the character hill. And second, community transference has to occur. An individual must join and continue to participate in a community supportive of his decision. He must walk away from the corrosive influence of his former community and join a like-minded community of support.

Man Up, Own Up, and Climb Up

One of the most important things I can communicate to you about character is this: Your character is determined not by whether you ever make a mistake, but by what you do about it. Let me say it again. Your character—or the character of your company or organization or family—is not determined by whether you mess up, but by what you do to own up to your mistake and repair the damage you have caused.

Everybody is going to mess up now and then. We all understand that, and most of us don't expect those around us to be perfect. We just want the person who made the mistake to stop the action and do something to right the wrong.

When you blow it, do you run and hide, pretending the incident never happened? Do you maintain a position of plausible deniability? Do you point the finger at someone else? Or do you man up, step up, and fess up?

Conclusion

In response to one of my Facebook posts about character, someone once commented that either you're born with it or you're not. I couldn't disagree more. Character is well within the exercise of the Power of Choice. Character is something you build. It is something you can always improve. If your character is damaged, you can repair it. If it is weak, you can strengthen it. Character is the most subtle of the Seven Powers but also one of the most important. Never underestimate its importance. Always value its significance.

POWER OF CHARACTER APPLICATION QUESTIONS—
Inspecting Your Character Frame

1. Would your family and coworkers describe your character as excellent, adequate, or deficient?

2. Name three areas of your character that most people who know you would say are excellent.

3. Name three areas of your character that most people who know you would say need strengthening.

4. What one thing would you change about your character? What do you need to do to make that change?

GROUP DISCUSSION QUESTIONS

1. Relate a story of when you have taken a stand for right even though it wasn't the popular choice.

2. Whose character do you most admire and why?

3. What would you like people to say about your character when you're not around?

7

The Power of
BELIEF

//

In the 1996 movie *Phenomenon*, John Travolta plays George Malley, a simple, good-hearted car mechanic living in a small town in Northern California. After attending his birthday celebration at a local tavern, George walks outside, looks up at the stars, and is hit with a blinding flash of light.

Shortly afterward, George discovers he has amazing new mental capabilities that allow him to absorb and process information at an exponential rate. When he develops telekinetic and psychic powers, he tries to retain some normalcy in his life while exploring his new abilities.

In the meantime, George attempts to woo a skittish single mom named Lace Pennamin (Kyra Sedgwick), who has a thriving small business selling handcrafted grapevine chairs at George's repair shop. Unbeknownst to Lace, George is her best customer, buying most of her chairs so that he will continue to have opportunities to see her.

In the movie's third act, George's health declines, and he is hospitalized as doctors research his condition. Meanwhile, George's longtime friend and confidant Doc Brunder (Robert Duvall) sits in the town tavern, quietly contemplating the fate of his friend, and he overhears some of the townsfolk speaking ill of George and his spooky new abilities.

Doc derails the criticism by asking one of George's detractors named Banes (Sean O'Bryan) how his relationship with his girlfriend, Lisa, is going. Caught off guard, Banes answers that he and his girlfriend have broken up. Doc commiserates with Banes for a moment before telling him that George's relationship with Lace is going very well. The explanation Doc offers for George's healthy relationship is that George buys Lace's chairs. Then Doc asks Banes if he has ever bought Lisa's chairs. He goes on to tell Banes that every woman has something she invests herself in, and he asks Banes if he has ever figured out what Lisa's chairs are and bought them.

Are you in the habit of buying the chairs of your loved ones? Do you buy the chairs of the organizations to which you belong? Do you buy your own chairs? Does anyone else buy your chairs?

All of us need people to buy into who we are and what we're about.

Gas Station Attendant or Governor?

The story goes that a governor and his wife were touring the state, campaigning for his reelection, when their limousine driver announced that they were low on gas. As they pulled off the highway into a small country gas station, the governor and his wife noticed they were back in the town where they had grown up, met, and married.

As the gas station attendant ambled out to the car, the governor said to his wife, "Hey, isn't that your old boyfriend pumping our gas?"

The governor's wife looked out the window for a moment and then said, "Why, yes, I believe it is."

"Just think," the governor said in a smug tone, "if you had married him instead of me, you would have been the wife of a gas station attendant."

"Just think," his wife replied without missing a beat, "if I had married him, he would have been governor."

I don't know any married woman who doesn't like that joke. The underlying point is that no one makes it to the top on his own. It's impossible to name anyone who has been successful on their own. Shoot, even the Lone Ranger had Tonto, right? We all need people to believe in us, to invest in us, to support us if we are to move forward.

In turn, we all need to believe in the lives of those around us and invest in them. And if we are to function successfully, we all need to believe in the soundness of the world in which we dwell.

The Engine of Your Success Vehicle

There is a reason the Power of Belief is last in the list of the Seven Powers. Not that it's the least important, because it's not. It's very important. I wouldn't call it the engine of your success vehicle if it didn't matter. The reason it's placed at the end of the list is that for years our society has placed it foremost among all motivational principles.

Our educational system has told us that we can do anything if we just believe in ourselves. Religious leaders have told us that if we just believe hard enough we can make anything happen. Politicians running for office have asked us to believe in change. Motivational speakers have told us that we can be rich and successful if we just believe.

The whole world is screaming at us to believe. But belief by itself does nothing. Try going out to your garage and sitting on a car engine and see if that gets you anywhere. Belief is power, but power must be channeled for it to be effective. For the Power of Belief to function, you must channel it through the other six of the Seven Powers. You need the whole success vehicle to get you where you want to go.

But your success vehicle isn't going anywhere without an engine, either. The Power of Belief has three components:

- belief in yourself—an unyielding, dogged conviction in your innermost being that you can and you will

- belief in other people—a passionate, expressed support and investment in the lives of the people around you

- belief in your world—a foundational faith that the constructs of this universe are sound and dependable

If you don't believe in yourself, you'll have a hard time being motivated to get out of bed and off to work. If you don't believe in the other members of your team, you'll struggle to motivate them to move in the right direction. If you don't believe in your world, it won't be easy for you to conceptualize solutions to take you and your organization forward.

You have to have a strong element of belief in order to get from point A to point B. If one of the three components of the Power of Belief is deficient, your belief engine will not function properly. You might get down the road a bit, but will you get as far as you want to go, as fast as you want to get there? Remember, success is defined as fulfilling your potential. How well does your belief engine run?

Belief Defined

Believing is not wishing, it is not hoping, it is not imagining. Belief is a universal power that at times defies logic. It is a firm resolve in the face of certain defeat. It is a bold confidence beyond rational explanation. It is an assurance of the unseen, in the not yet manifested.

Belief can be counterfeited and imitated, but there is no substitute for it. There can be an external show of belief without an internal witness. Before anything comes into existence, there must be belief. Before you start a business, before you get your degree, before any miracle, before any journey, before any successful transition, there must be belief.

Belief is knowing because you know. It is the conviction that precedes the understanding. It is sometimes quiet and sometimes loud but always bold. It is tenaciously holding on and moving forward when doubt is screaming in your ear. It is an inner calm when disaster looms.

Belief is not an emotion. It is not a feeling. It can walk beside either dismay or elation without being swayed. It can stand against the winds of despair and jubilance and not be moved. And like any other force of the universe, it has rules.

- Belief is a universal law. It is an intangible, powerful force that can either elevate or destroy. As I mentioned in chapter 3, what you believe about yourself will determine what you believe is possible in your life. In this chapter, I'm looking at what is possible if you believe in yourself, the people around you, and your world.

- Belief has to be attached to something. You can't just believe. You have to believe in something or someone— God, your business, yourself, the government, your product, your kids, your country, your creed…It's impossible to say "I believe" without associating that belief with a person, object, or concept.

- All belief is not equal. Even when belief is directed toward the same idea, some people believe more strongly in that idea than others. Equal claims to belief do not necessarily reflect equal belief.

- A belief can only be as strong as the object to which it is attached. Belief in the eternal will always prove stronger than belief in the temporal.

HERE'S A THOUGHT…

It takes no belief to acknowledge the sun is shining on a cloudless day.

- Belief must be expressed. You can't say you believe in someone but never show it. Whether in the divine or the ordinary, belief unexpressed is theoretical at best.

- If you're not doing it, you don't believe it. Have you bought in to your religion, your career, your family? Do you truly believe?

Rational Versus Irrational Belief

What is irrational belief? Sometimes that's an easy question to answer. Let's say, for example, that you believe you're going to have breakfast on Jupiter tomorrow morning, or that you're going to grow a third arm this afternoon. I'd have to throw those beliefs in the irrational category.

But what if you believe you can become a major-league pitcher? Well, sure, I guess, if you are young enough and have the talent, ability, and discipline, then I'd say that might be a rational belief. But would it be a rational belief if doctors told you that you were missing the one essential ligament every pitcher needs to stabilize his arm enough to throw a baseball? No, that would absolutely not be rational.

Well, hold on a minute. It may be a rational belief if you have the drive and determination of R.A. Dickey.

R.A. Dickey is known all over the world as the National League 2012 Cy Young Award winner and a master of baseball's toughest pitch, the knuckleball. After a successful amateur baseball career in high school and college, Dickey was set to begin his professional career pitching for the Texas Rangers, which came with an $810,000 signing bonus.

During the routine physical exam before he signed, doctors discovered that Dickey's throwing arm lacked an ulnar collateral ligament. The UCL is a triangular ligament in the elbow that stabilizes the arm, and it's considered indispensable to a pitcher. The discovery spooked the Rangers, and they retracted their original offer, along with the hefty signing bonus.

A short while later, Dickey accepted a greatly reduced offer of $75,000 from the Rangers and began his long and arduous baseball career. For years, Dickey slogged his way through the minor leagues, turning in far too few admirable performances to earn him his place in the majors. As the years began to pile on, Dickey realized that he needed to improve if he were to stay in the game. He committed to developing his ability to throw the rare and elusive knuckleball pitch, seeking help and advice from veteran knuckleballers, such as Phil Niekro and Charlie Hough.

Dickey's investment in his craft reached a zenith with his record-breaking 2012 season with the New York Mets. In December of 2012, the 38-year-old pitcher, whom everyone had dismissed, reached an agreement with the Toronto Blue Jays for a two-year contract extension worth $25 million.

R.A. Dickey and other boundary-breakers like him make the distinction between the rational and the irrational difficult. Sure, there are some folks that are clearly divorced from reality and believe that they're Mayor McCheese. But there is a mighty big area in between the rational and irrational that is hard to label.

So who am I to tell you whether your belief is irrational? It might seem that way to me, but you might know something about your situation that I don't. You might be the one to break the barriers and define your own reality.

Believe in Yourself

There are times in your success journey when you conceive a vision and choose to pursue it. You create solutions for your problem and attempt to act on your vision and implement positive change. But there is just one problem. No one gets your vision. Nobody sees what you see.

- You want to buy and remodel a distressed property for resale, but your spouse can't envision the finished product and therefore isn't in agreement with the purchase.

- You want to go to school to get your degree so you can get a better-paying job, but no one in your family has ever gone to college, so you are belittled and scorned for your ambition.

- You want to go into business for yourself, but the people around you just can't see you as a businessman.

- You want to get in shape, and you've started running. You're up to two miles a day, and you're considering training to run in a marathon. But your family and friends laugh at the idea.

Sometimes, when you get a new vision for your life or organization, the people around you don't see things the way you do. They want to know, who do you think you are, getting such ideas? You're putting on airs, rising above your station in life. You should be satisfied with the way things are and quit bothering everyone around you with your foolish notions.

It's really not their fault. They see you or your project as it is now, and you see things as they could be. They see you, your body, your circumstance, or your organization with the eyes of yesterday, and you see with the eyes of tomorrow. You each have a unique perspective of reality. Once you begin envisioning your goal as possible and attainable, conflict will naturally arise between you and those who view your vision as impossible. You are assaulting their view of reality, and they will fight back.

Welcome to the life of the visionary. Sometimes you can feel as if you're on your own with no support, encouragement, or assistance. Even worse, by just daring to think differently, you may have unwittingly created adversaries within your own camp. Change threatens people. The people in your family or community might be comfortable seeing you as you currently are. You and your circumstances don't challenge or threaten them. For you to aspire to be more, to do something different, to make something more of yourself, can be very threatening to those around you. They might feel in danger of being left behind, losing you, or being looked down up on.

Or perhaps you haven't done a very good job of selling your vision to the people around you. Maybe you haven't painted a picture of what the end will look like.

Or maybe you have painted the picture, but still no one seems to be getting behind your vision. Nobody sees how great your idea is or how wonderful it will be after you complete your project. What do you do now? You have a choice in front of you. You can either buy into the reality that a few other people have for your life, or you can choose to believe in yourself anyway.

Crazy Publishing Story

In 2006, my wife and I were discussing the idea of me attending a writers' conference. We agreed it would be a great way for me to meet some folks in the publishing industry and learn a bit about how it worked. So when we noticed that I was booked to speak in a town where a big writers' conference was being held, all that was left for me to do was register for the conference and write them a check.

I hadn't attended this type of event before, so I was looking forward to meeting other writers and diving into the world of publishing. One of the features of this conference was that attendees could bring their book proposals and have publishers and editors critique them. I brought my book proposal with me and, like everyone else, hoped I would get some positive feedback and maybe a little bit of interest from a publisher. My proposal was for *I'm Not Crazy, but I Might Be a Carrier,* an inspirational compilation of 40 of my best humor columns. I thought it was a great idea for a book, but I didn't let myself get too worked up about finding a publisher for it at this conference. I realized I was a rookie and had a lot to learn, so I decided to relax and enjoy the experience.

During my time there, I met a lot of great people and got some helpful information. Most of the people I met were very encouraging and had upbeat perspectives. A couple of folks, though, did their best to pummel any stray optimism that happened to be floating around the room.

One woman shook her head dismissively when she learned it was my first time there. "Well, don't get your hopes up," she said. "I had to attend these things for five years before I ever got a book contract. Then, after you find a publisher, it'll be at least another year or two before your book is published, if it ever is at all."

Because I'm the crack mathematician that I am, I was able to add the five and two together almost instantly, and I realized she believed I wouldn't see anything of mine on the bookstore shelves for at least another seven years. I smiled and thanked her for her input, and she said she hoped it helped. Thank God, I didn't take it to heart. Long ago, I programmed a secret bit of code in my mind called "You don't know what I know."

For years I had received positive feedback on my syndicated humor column, so I knew people really liked my pieces. I also knew there was some good buzz about my book floating around the conference. But even so, some industry people weren't sold on the concept.

"This book just won't sell," one editor told me. "People don't want inspiration right after they've been reading humor. It just doesn't work." Never mind that the material had been working well in my syndicated column for years and that it was a compilation of the best of the best of those columns. When I heard the doomsayers tell me the book would never sell, I just thanked them for their input, referred to my "You don't know what I know" programming, and went on my way. About a month later, a publisher sent me an offer. It wasn't a huge offer, but the book sold.

There are times on your journey when no one around you seems to believe in you. No one sees your vision. Nobody gets what you're trying to accomplish. No one thinks you can make it happen. How you respond to the naysayers will depend largely on your level of self-belief. All innovators have to believe in themselves, not only when the sky is clear but also when the winds of doubt are battering their vision.

If you are to move forward, fulfill your potential, and complete your vision, you must invest in yourself. You must be the one person who continues to believe when no one else seems to.

The Dos and Don'ts of Self-Investment

Do Find a Support Community

In chapter 1, I suggested you give some thought to building your support community. Do you have a group of people around you who support you as you undertake new challenges? Do they lift you up when you are struggling? Do they encourage you when you are weak?

As I mentioned earlier in this chapter, no man is an island, and there is no such thing as the Lone Ranger. No astronaut ever made it to the moon by himself. No race car driver makes it to the finish line without a crew. If you are going to expand your horizons, accomplish new things, and explore your potential, you need to surround yourself with people who will help you get where you are going. You need people who believe in you, who are invested in your success.

Do Find a Mentor

Your community should include at least one mentor—someone who believes in you and is willing to offer the benefit of his or her wisdom and knowledge. That person should have a good deal of experience in the area in which you wish to grow. It's great if your mentor has ten years of experience, but it's fantastic if he has forty. The more, the better. It also helps if your mentor is still active in the area in which you wish to learn. Our times are rapidly changing, and what worked ten years ago might not necessarily be applicable today.

I cannot state this strongly enough: Your mentor should be of the same gender as you so there is no temptation of romantic entanglement. Many people discount this foundational rule only to regret it later. A mentor and protégé spend a lot of one-on-one time together. It's much better to eliminate any chance of misstep before temptation arises than to try to make up your mind about it when it's camped on your front doorstep.

You can find a mentor almost anywhere—at work, in the local chamber of commerce or a professional association, or in your church or neighborhood. Anyplace where quality people are likely to congregate can produce a mentor for you.

Don't wait for your mentor to ask you if you would like to be his protégé. Take the initiative, employ the Power of Action, and make the move yourself. I don't know anyone who wouldn't be flattered and want to help someone who approached him and said, "I really admire what you've been able to accomplish in our industry, and I feel I could learn a lot from you. Would you be able to meet with me for coffee next week? I'd like to hear whatever you would like to teach me."

Don't Share Your Vision with Everybody

When you first conceive your idea, endeavor, or enterprise, it is young and vulnerable. It needs nurture and support. It needs a safe place to grow, away from scrutiny and critique. There will be a time for evaluation and analysis later as it grows and develops, but not at first. Your new project or goal must survive its infancy.

How many times have you shared a great idea with someone who shot it down immediately? How likely are you to continue to pursue an idea if the first few people who hear about it think it's awful?

When your idea, plan, or vision is young, it is crucial that you share it only with people who will accept and support you. Of course, you need advisors to help you refine your idea further down the road, but when it's a newborn concept, guard and protect it. Just for a little while. Sit on your idea for a bit and ruminate on it. Get comfortable with your level of commitment to the idea or pursuit before announcing it to the world.

Only after you thoroughly know it and own it should you announce it.

Do Read Motivational and Inspirational Books

Everyone needs encouragement. We like to pretend we don't. We would like to see ourselves as self-sufficient and independent, but we are neither. People need encouragement like plants need water, but if that encouragement isn't available from the person standing next to you, what are you to do?

I like to think that thousands of voices are just waiting to encourage me. They're residing on bookshelves everywhere. Earlier in this book, I encouraged you to take hold of your programming by reading, and a large part of that programming is reading books that feed your soul.

Countless times when I have struggled with the challenges in front of me, my wife has brought me a book that either educated me about the area I was struggling in or encouraged me with tales of people who fought personal battles and triumphed. When you read about another person who was able to gain victory in his life, that story has the power to ignite the flame of belief in you. If one person can slay his dragon, you can overcome yours.

I often use the phrase "When it *seems* no one else believes in you" because rare indeed are the instances in our lives when truly not one person believes in us. Still, at times, we can certainly feel that way, can't we? I can't tell you all the times when I seemed to be standing bloodied and battered in my corner with no one rooting for me. In fact, I can even tell you about a few times when everyone in the room seemed to be cheering for my opponent.

Those times are inevitable. If you are going to be different, try something new, and improve, you should get ready for times of isolation and challenge. Better yet, prepare yourself for them by fortifying yourself with enough strength so you can weather the storm. Don't wait until the storm hits before you buy insurance. Don't wait until you run out of gas before you fill up. Invest in your self-belief now, when the sky is blue and the winds are fair.

What motivational or inspirational books would be best for you to read? That question has no right or wrong answer. I suggest you read whatever works for you. Find a mine shaft that is rich and tunnel as far as it will take you.

What do I like, you ask? I mentioned earlier that I find biographies particularly uplifting. I also find it very encouraging to read the Bible, which is great anytime but especially when times are tough. I am always mentioning books that I enjoy on Facebook, so look me up at www.facebook.com/charlesmarshallspeaks and hit the "like" button if you would like a few more direct suggestions.

Believe in the People Around You

Ben was a problem waiting to happen. One day when he was young, his anger with a boy in his neighborhood reached a boiling point, so he pulled out his camping knife and plunged it toward the boy's abdomen. Fortunately, the blade tip hit the boy's large metal belt buckle, and the knife blade broke. The boys parted afterward, and the incident went no further.

Nothing about Ben's early life marked him for success. Raised in an impoverished, single-parent home in Detroit, Ben appeared to be destined to become another statistic, another brief, tragic mention on the evening news as either victim or perpetrator.

It's ironic that Ben came so close to becoming a murderer in the way that he did, because years later, his skill with a blade would propel him to worldwide recognition, renown, and respect. But that fame was in the distant future, and Ben's success was anything but certain. Still, Ben had a secret weapon that would prove bigger than his poverty, bigger than the odds that were stacked against him, bigger than his poor self-image.

In his early years, Ben was a poor student and came to think of himself as unintelligent. When his mother saw his report card in fifth grade, she was horrified. Having only a third-grade education herself, she feared her son was repeating her mistakes and heading toward a life of hardship. Having no idea what to do, she prayed for wisdom and came up with a plan.

She would allow her sons to watch only two hours of preselected television a week. She also started her sons on a reading program with the Detroit Public Library and required them to submit regular book reports to her. At that time, her sons didn't know that due to her limited education, she was unable to read them. She hid her inability from her sons by acting as though she were reading the reports and then placing small check marks on each one when she was finished.

Ben's mom refused to accept any excuses from her sons. Her attitude was that if you have a brain, you can find an answer. As a result, Ben and his brother became excellent problem solvers.

Ben's mother continued to invest in him and challenge him to excel throughout high school, college, and medical school. In 1987, Dr. Ben Carson made history by becoming the first surgeon to successfully separate twins conjoined at the head. Dr. Carson is now the director of pediatric neurosurgery at Johns Hopkins Hospital, and in 2008, he was awarded the Presidential Medal of Freedom by President George W. Bush.

What was Ben's secret weapon in overcoming all the challenges he faced? The belief and support of his mother. In view of the many people in his high school who died early deaths, Dr. Carson believes he probably wouldn't even be alive today if not for his mother's efforts. Dr. Carson also gives credit for his success to a number of teachers who went the extra mile, giving him additional instruction and tutoring after class hours.

How important is it to believe and invest in the lives of the people in your life? Sometimes, your support can mean the difference between life and death.

In my presentation "Real Heroes Don't Wear Spandex," I make the point that real heroes aren't celebrities, movie stars, or professional athletes. In real life, heroes are people who make a difference with their lives by investing those around them. You don't need to magically morph into Florence Nightingale or Mother Teresa to make a difference in the world. You only need to intentionally, positively impact the lives of those in your immediate circle of influence.

I shudder to think where I might have wound up if not for the investment of kindhearted people along the way. People who have no idea how much they meant to my success. People who were just being themselves. People who were fulfilling their mission of making a contribution.

A Hero You've Never Heard Of

As I mentioned earlier in this book, junior high school was not a happy place for me. This is true for most people I know unless they had the status that comes from wealth, good looks, or special skills, such as athletic ability. I had none of those things. Certainly not the money.

My family's finances were already hurting because of some missteps my father had made in the insurance business. But then things got exponentially worse when my father limped home from a business trip after barely surviving a heart attack. He had been dining in a Dallas restaurant when he felt intense chest pains and fell to the floor, clutching his chest, gasping for air. A man at an adjacent table noticed his distress and leapt into action, immediately administering CPR. I'm so thankful that stranger applied the Power of Action, because I can't imagine how hard it would have been for my family if my father had died that day.

I don't know why Dad was recuperating at home instead of the hospital. I suppose it had something to do with our being poor. But it was a scary time at our house. The whole house was dark and deathly quiet. My father was sequestered in the back bedroom when my mother gathered all of us children together and told us that Daddy had a heart attack and was very, very sick. She told us we needed to pray that God would have mercy and let our daddy live. A couple of days later I was looking for a bit of reassurance to ease my anxiety, so I asked Mom if she thought Dad would live. I remember she still had no comfort to offer, saying with tears in her eyes, "I don't know, son. I just don't know."

My father slowly got better but was unable to work. Mom, who until then had been a stay-at-home mother of five, had to get a job as an office manager at Gibson's Department Store just to put food on the table. There were a lot of nights that we ate Kraft macaroni and cheese, and to tell you the truth, I never noticed any big difference in our finances. The only time I felt the sting of not having money was at school, where everything had suddenly become all about looks, status, and money, all of which I didn't have.

It was just before middle school that I saw Mr. Mullins for the first time. I was attending my older sister's choir concert in the school auditorium and noticed a drum set just to the left of the stage. Before the performance began, the choir director announced that the school's new band director would accompany the choir on his drum set.

I don't think I heard a note the choir sang that night. All I remember is watching Mr. Mullins play those drums. I was mesmerized by every beat, every stroke he played. That, I thought, is what I want to do.

When our principal announced band tryouts a week later, I was one of the first ones in line. After passing a basic tonality test, about 90 other kids and I had to endure six weeks of music theory class before we could try out for the instruments we wanted to play. I tried out for the drums and performed horribly. I still wanted to be in the band though, so Mr. Mullins suggested that I play a school-supplied instrument, such as a tuba or a baritone, since my family couldn't afford to buy an instrument for me. I reluctantly agreed to play the baritone and faithfully hauled that thing in its musty old case back and forth to school every day. I even practiced regularly even though I had no passion for it.

I made it all the way through sixth grade playing the baritone, but a month into my seventh-grade year, I knew I couldn't hack it anymore. My dream was to play the drums, and if I couldn't play the drums, well, I didn't want to play anything. I mustered up the courage and went to speak to Mr. Mullins. I told him about my frustrations and I told him about my dream to play the drums. I didn't tell him about the hard time I was having at home or the incessant teasing I was getting at school. I probably didn't have to because it must have been pretty obvious.

I don't know if he gave me a second chance to try out on the drums out of pity or if he was just doing his job, but I do know that I'll be forever grateful that he did.

Mr. Mullins's office was only slightly larger than a Gemini space capsule. Stacks of sheet music and various instrument parts, tools, and music stands filled what little space there was. Standing at the edge of his desk, Mr. Mullins placed a pair of drumsticks in my hands and showed me how to hold them properly. To the best of my knowledge, it was the first time I had ever held a pair of drumsticks in my life. He told me that he was going to tap out a rhythm on the corner of his desk and that I was supposed to duplicate the pattern immediately afterward.

I don't know if I stood there for five minutes or for an hour. One by one, Mr. Mullins drummed rhythm after rhythm, and one by one, I repeated them. When we finished, Mr. Mullins smiled and asked me a few questions about my desire to play drums, and that was the end of my tryout. I had no idea whether I had passed or failed miserably.

My mother was standing at the door waiting for me when I got home. "What on earth did you do?" she asked.

I didn't know what she was talking about, but I figured I must have screwed up pretty royally for her to be as worked up as she was. "I don't know, Mama," I replied. "What's wrong?"

"Wrong?" my mother asked, surprised. "Nothing's wrong. I just got off the phone with Mr. Mullins, and he went on and on about how you were born to play the drums. He said we need to get you started playing right away!"

A mixture of surprise, pleasure, and relief swept over me. And also anxiety. I knew we had no money and that buying a drum wasn't likely. A new drum would cost well over $100, but it may as well have been $1000 because we didn't have it. Period. But the way my mother was carrying on about the things Mr. Mullins had said about me…well, just maybe…

My mom must have done quite a sales job on my dad because before you could say "Buddy Rich," I was standing at the counter at Werlein's Music in downtown Jackson, Mississippi. My parents had made an arrangement with the store to buy a brand-spanking-new Ludwig concert snare drum with a practice pad, size 2B drumsticks, and a case for somewhere in the neighborhood of $125. They came up with a bit of money to put down on the purchase and then agreed to pay something like $5 or $10 a month.

Two or three weeks later, I was first chair of the drum section.

Suddenly I was no longer just a geek at school. I was a geek who played the drums! Kids still made fun of me, but now I had a niche and a place in the order of things. It bolstered my self-esteem, and since Mr. Mullins had believed in me, I dared to believe in myself, if only just a tiny bit. I can't begin to tell you how much playing the drums helped me get through those tough years. I can't begin to tell you how much Mr. Mullins's belief in me jump-started my belief in myself. I would certainly continue to have trouble at home and school, but just one person taking the time to invest in my life had altered my outlook and prospects.

With Thanks to Paul Harvey, the Rest of the Story

I have traveled all over the country and told this story probably hundreds of times. Not long ago I asked my wife if I had ever mentioned Mr. Mullins's speech difficulties.

"No," she answered. "I don't think so. What do you mean?"

"Mr. Mullins had a stuttering problem," I said.

"Really? How bad was it?"

"Well, it was kind of bad," I said. "He had a real tough time having a normal conversation. The stuttering showed up mostly when he was talking to adults, but it also happened when he was directing band. Sometimes he would get frustrated at students talking to each other instead of listening to him or not paying attention to his directing, and the stutter would manifest itself in a big way. When we had band concerts, he would have a student or another faculty member announce the program. He almost never spoke to an audience himself."

"Wow," my wife said, taking it all in. "No, you never mentioned that to me." A moment passed, and then she said, "That seems pretty important. Why is it that you never told me about Mr. Mullins's speech impediment?"

I thought about that for a moment and then replied, "Because it just never seemed that important."

When I think about the enormous way Mr. Mullins impacted my life—the way he invested in me, believed in me, and thus helped shape the person I am today—any external characteristic, such how tall he was, what kind of glasses he wore, or the way he spoke, doesn't make one bit of difference to me. All that matters to me is that somebody cared enough to reach out and plant a seed of belief in a nerdy little junior high school kid. And that nerdy kid remembers that investment to this day.

The Dos and Don'ts of Investment in Others

Do Be a Mentor

Of course you can be a mentor! Everyone has something to offer, and you would be shortchanging your community if you didn't offer a bit of your knowledge to those around you. The funny thing is, you might already be mentoring people and not even know it. Mentors rarely wear badges that say, Hello, I'm a Mentor. Mentorship is usually the subtle influence of senior team members offering wisdom, either by word or deed, to younger, less experienced members of their team.

If you are a parent, you have a built-in daily opportunity to impact your kids' lives. Most parents live adjacent to their kids, occupying the same living space but never making an attempt to connect with them on a daily basis. Mentoring a child isn't about showing up to take them to the zoo or give them a lecture. It's about kids and adults hanging out and sharing each other's lives.

Here are three things you're going to need to know to get started being a mentor.

1. A mentor has to be relevant. If you and your input are not relevant to your protégé's world, your impact will be minimal.

2. A mentor must first listen to his protégé. You can't pre-scribe a cure if you haven't bothered to do an examination.

3. A mentor has to spend time with his protégé. If you want to impact young people's lives, they need to see you in regular, everyday action.

Mentoring is an essential part of your growth that cannot be attained by any other means. You can learn some lessons only by teaching other people.

Do Give Books Away

In my first book, *Shattering the Glass Slipper*, I explore what might happen to Cinderella if she lived in the real world instead of a fairy-tale world. What would her options be if her fairy godmother never showed up? Instead of magic coming to her rescue, I imagine that Cinderella is given an old book that contains the Seven Powers of Success. She discovers principles in the book that she uses to create a way out of her dilemma and into her dreams. At the end of the tale, Cinderella passes along her knowledge by giving away the very book she was given years earlier.

Books shouldn't die. They shouldn't wind up on someone's dusty bookshelf unused and unwanted. Books were meant to be passed on. A book's job isn't finished until its binding is falling apart and pages are crumbling.

If a book inspires you, read it and give it away. Then go buy ten or fifteen copies of it and give them to your friends. If a book inspired you, you can use it to inspire other people. Post your thoughts about it on Facebook and Twitter. Tell your family, tell your friends, tell the world—change the world.

Don't Be a Phony

When I ask you to believe in people, I'm not asking you to lie. People sometimes object to my encouragement to believe in the people around them, essentially saying, "But Charles, the people on my team are idiots! Do you want me to lie to them?" Not at all. I'm not asking you to tell anyone anything that isn't true. I'm simply asking you to communicate to those around you that you believe they have what it takes to overcome the challenges they have before them. There is a huge difference between believing in people and believing in their abilities. I'm asking you to communicate to those around you that you believe they have what it takes to move through and beyond the challenges they are presently facing.

Do Speak Up

It's not the Power of Belief if you don't act on it. For the Power of Belief to come alive, it must be verbally expressed. That's *verbally* expressed. There is no excuse for not communicating positivity to the people around you. I've heard all the excuses before. "I'm just not a verbal person." "I express my feelings through actions." "People already know what I think." "I said it all a while back." No excuse works as a cop-out for choosing not to verbally give to those around you.

Often when I'm speaking to groups about the Power of Belief, I do an exercise that underscores and reinforces the Power of Belief in attendees' lives. I have my audience break up into groups of three to five people. Then one by one, each person makes a positive comment about the other people in his group. It doesn't matter if some people in the group don't know one another. The task remains the same—observe and comment on one positive thing you see in another person. The objective is for every person to practice building up another person with his words and to allow other people to build him up in return.

The difference between people's faces before and after the exercise is amazing. When we finish the exercise, every face in the room is glowing. There is a new energy in the room, and everyone seems refreshed and renewed.

Such is the Power of Belief.

If you want to have some fun without waiting for a humorous speaker to come to town, try this little experiment the next time you're in the grocery store. When you're ready to check out, choose the checkout line with the most sullen cashier. Watch that cashier's interaction with every person ahead of you in the line. When it's your turn to check out, greet the cashier with a bright hello and call her by the name on her name tag. Compliment her about something she's doing right (make sure it's an appropriate comment)—her professionalism, her nails, her smile, or anything else. Then watch how she greets the next person in line. I guarantee that you will see an increase in her energy level and enthusiasm. I've done this dozens of times and have never seen it fail.

You have incredible power at your disposal. You have the ability to change the world around you for the better. Why wouldn't you want to bring this kind of energy to the people on your team? Why wouldn't you want to create enthusiasm and energy at your workplace? Why wouldn't you want to be someone's hero?

Believe in Your World

It seemed everyone I spoke with in 1999 was talking about the upcoming year and how it might affect computers all over the world. The concern was that most computer software at that time had been written to keep the date in the 1900s. Many experts believed that when the clock turned from 11:59 p.m. 1999 to 12:00 a.m. 2000, there was a real possibility that the programs would malfunction, causing chaos in system operations in almost every facet of our society. Power grids would go out, causing people in cities to have no means of buying food or conducting business. Communication would shut down, meaning no land lines or cell phones would work, so if people had fire, medical, or police emergencies, they would be out of luck. Financial records would be irrevocably lost. Medical records would vanish. In essence, we would all be reduced to living like cavemen. People would riot, and lawlessness would ensue. Some people predicted the end of all things— a global, societal meltdown.

As the hour in question approached, people speculated with one another about what might happen. Would there be any glitches? How bad would they be? What was the extent of everyone's Y2K preparation? Who had food-storage lockers, and were they filled? Who had bought enough ammunition to stave off the crowds of roaming pillagers? Some of these questions seem silly now, but in 1999, industries that supported survivalists flourished.

Sometimes the Y2K topic was discussed on television and radio talk shows, but most of the time these conversations were held just

under the surface—at the mailbox, at the kids' baseball game, at dinner with friends.

I don't need to tell you the rest of the story. The clock hit 12, people in Times Square said hooray and kissed each other, and that was
about it. Don't get me wrong. Success is never accidental. There was a
lot of work that went into making sure systems were Y2K compliant,
and because of that effort and the foresight of those in leadership, we
were all just fine.

Not the First Time, Not the Last

Y2K wasn't the first time that type of fear had spread. It was going
on long before I was born and will continue long after I'm gone. The
reasons for these seasons of fear vary. Some are more valid than others. In World War II, many people in the United States lived in constant fear of an attack on the 48 contiguous states. During that time,
San Francisco was bristling with underwater minefields and shoreline
gun batteries. You can still see the remains of this vast defense network
today. People lived under a very real threat of invasion or attack, and
fear was rampant.

Then came the atomic bomb and an awareness of our vulnerabil-
ity in the case of an attack by the Russians. People built bomb shelters
in their backyards and stocked them with supplies. Dozens of smaller
national waves of fear have come and gone since then. Even now, as
I write this book, a significant number of people are preparing for a
doomsday event based on the close of the Mayan calendar. That theory
goes that because the Mayan calendar ends on December 21, 2012, the
Mayans must have known something we don't (the world is going to
end). If they hadn't known this, obviously they would have continued
their calendar, right? But since they didn't, the whole world is going to
suffer a cataclysmic event on or around that date. Right now, people
are building and selling luxury doomsday apartments in underground
bunkers that are provisioned with food and water and a small arsenal.
Some people's entire existence is built on the belief that the sky will
soon fall and that we're all going to die.

Where Do You Want to Land?

What is your reaction when you hear of "wars and rumors of wars"? How quickly do you accept such beliefs? What about warnings of impending economic doom? What do you feel in your heart when pundits make dire forecasts for our economy? How about climate change? What is your reaction to the frequent news reports of the earth changing?

I don't have any problem with people acting responsibly to care for themselves and their families. I'm all for folks employing the Power of Action to improve their situation and protect themselves. But I do have a problem with people panicking and designing their lives around the fear of death and destruction. I don't want to be that kind of person. Do you? If I build my world around fear, then fear has already won. If I am more invested in saving my life than in living it, my life has become centered on death, not life.

How you see the world and what you believe about it will determine how you interact with it. If you see this world as a place of hope, optimism, and opportunity, you are more likely to take the risks that lead to discovery and success. If you see the world as a dark, dangerous, and treacherous place, you might react by acting defensively. You might not be shopping for a doomsday bunker, but let me ask you, do any of the following phrases ever pass through your mind?

> My boss is out to get me.
>
> Nothing ever goes my way.
>
> God will never let me succeed.
>
> I am destined for failure.
>
> Nobody likes me.
>
> I always have to do everybody else's job.
>
> There is no God. We're a product of universal chance.
>
> I'm not paid what I'm worth.

If so, may I suggest that you might not be believing in your world?

Rather than believing in the good in your world, you are reinforcing your belief in the bad in your world.

Yes, there is bad in the world, but that doesn't mean your reaction automatically has to be defensive or hostile. Some people see the same bad things you do, but they have a completely different reaction. Because of their belief system, they see the darkness in the world and conclude that the world needs heroes, so they get busy trying to do something to help other people.

Which Is It Going to Be?

Each of us has a decision to make. Will we build a belief system based on fear of the possibility of evil? Or will we build a belief system built on faith in the possibility of good?

The World I Believe In

I believe that an armless girl can learn how to fly and get her pilot's license. Jessica Cox was born without arms in 1983 in Sierra Vista, Arizona. Her parents have invested the Power of Belief in Jessica, building her confidence and convincing her that she is capable of accomplishing anything she wants. She took dance lessons and danced for 14 years. She also took tae kwon do and earned her black belt when she was 14. In 2011, Jessica set a Guinness world record by being the first person to be certified to fly a plane using only her feet. Today she inspires people around the globe as an inspirational speaker.

I believe that a poor Filipino boy can grow up to become the lead singer in a world-famous rock band. Arnel Pineda was born in the Philippines on September 5, 1967. His mother died of a heart disease when Arnel was 13 years old, leaving the family impoverished. Shortly afterward, in order to ease his father's financial burden, Arnel moved out to live on his own. For two years he was virtually homeless, working odd jobs wherever he could so he could feed himself. In 1982, at the age of 15, Arnel joined his first band and began singing professionally. He worked as a rock singer for the next 25 years, working in various groups, playing cover versions of songs by bands such as Aerosmith, Led Zeppelin, and Journey. In 2007, Neal Schon, the lead guitarist of

Journey, saw a YouTube video featuring Arnel singing. That led to an audition with Journey, and Arnel eventually joined the band as their full-time lead vocalist.

I believe that a man born without arms or legs can become a world-famous inspirational speaker. Nicholas Vujicic was born in 1982 in Brisbane, Australia, with a rare affliction known as tetra-amelia syndrome, a condition that is characterized by the absence of all four limbs. Nick struggled early in his life and was picked on in school by other students because of his disability. This caused him to plunge into depression, and by the time he was eight years old, Nick began to consider suicide. Through prayer and the realization that he was not alone, that others struggle with similar difficulties, he began to make peace with his disability. Using only the two toes on his left foot (which is attached directly to his torso), Nick learned to write, use a computer (typing 43 words a minute), comb his hair, shave, swim, and perform a multitude of other tasks. Nick continued his education earning a double bachelor's degree in accounting and financial planning. Nick is now the president of Life Without Limbs and travels the world, sharing his belief that faith in God can transform our lives and give us meaning and purpose.

The Victor's Table

Sometimes I imagine myself sitting at dinner with a tableful of such people as these, hearing about the tremendous obstacles they've overcome to achieve the things they have. One by one they go around the table and tell their stories of the challenges they faced and the lessons they learned and applied to climb their own personal mountains. Then the conversation turns to me.

"Wow, Charles. You had the use of all your arms and legs. You were born in the United States, where opportunity abounds. You had access to some of the best schools in the world. You had the Internet to look up any information you wanted. So, what did you do with all of that?"

I'm still working on the answer to that question. I'd like to be able to say I didn't back up, back down, or back off. I'd like to say I gave the best I had to give. I'd like to say I fought a good fight. I'd like to hold my head up confidently and know that I belong at the table.

I believe all the people at that table have one thing in common: They all believe that this world is a place of opportunity and hope. Certainly they acknowledge the tremendous challenges before them, but they all face them bravely because their belief system supports the notion that they can achieve what they want if they apply themselves and persevere in the face of opposition.

Choosing Your Belief System

What about your belief system? You are responsible for constructing your own belief system, and you have chosen the one you currently hold. The way you see the world functioning around you, the way you see God, and the way you see other people are all constructs of your belief system.

Do you see the world as hostile or full of opportunity? Do you see other people as mostly helpful or hurtful? Do you see God as a mean, hateful, distant entity? Do you see him as a Santa Claus figure who will let you get away with almost anything? Or do you see him as a compassionate Father?

This is the most important advice I can give you about your belief system: Choose it carefully because you will become a product of that system. Your belief system comes down to this one thing: Are you a fear-based person or a faith-based person? All of us are afraid. All of us are in danger. But some people...well, some people charge into battle. Some people step out on the tight wire. Some people invest in a new business in a struggling economy. Some people get married when the divorce rate is skyrocketing.

Let me be found on the side of those who dare. Let me be counted among those who believe. Let me be seated at the table with those who have conquered.

POWER OF BELIEF APPLICATION QUESTIONS—
Tuning Up Your Belief Engine

1. Name one time you have believed in yourself and seen a project or goal through to completion without much external support.

2. Name three times in the past month when you have actively invested in the lives of those in your immediate circle.

3. Do people who know you see you as a supporter or detractor of their goals and plans?

4. Name one way in which you regularly nourish your Power of Belief.

GROUP ACTIVITY

Sitting in a circle, have all the group members identify something positive they see in all the other group members' lives, regardless of whether they know them well. See that everyone takes a turn both sharing and receiving.

Conclusion

I've spent a great deal of time and effort over the past ten or fifteen years trying to convince people that there is no magic in this world. No magic wands, no fairy dust, no fairy godmothers. The only magic is that which you create.

What we do have, though, I have given you. We have tools. If you use them, you can unlock your strengths and unleash your dreams. If you don't use them, they're just worthless implements gathering dust on the table of your life.

With every decision you make, every action you take, every conversation you have, you are writing the story of your life. Don't you want to know just how far this story can go? Wouldn't you like to find out what is possible with the protagonist in your story?

Every story needs a hero. Usually the hero is imperfect, has weaknesses, and feels that somebody else might be able to do the job better. Does that sound like anyone you know? You are that hero. You're the one who overcomes ridiculous odds, who dares the impossible, who is defeated but then rises again.

It might sound a bit melodramatic, but throw in some special effects and a love scene or two, and your life becomes a Hollywood movie. But your story has to have a good finish. I can't tell you the number of times I've had people come up to me after my program and say, "Hey, Charles, I've thought about writing a book."

"Oh, yeah? That's great! What's your book going to be about?" I usually respond.

"It's going to be about my life. I've been through some pretty amazing things."

"What kind of amazing things?" I ask.

"Oh, wow, where to start? Let's see. My wife divorced me fifteen years ago, and then I was in a car accident and almost got killed. Then I injured myself at work five years ago and went on disability."

"Man, that sounds like you've had some struggles," I say. "What did you do about those things?"

And that's where the amazing story usually peters out. Our hero had bad stuff happen to him just as every other person on the planet has, but at this point in his story, he hasn't risen above his challenges. His amazing story doesn't have an amazing ending—yet. It could eventually end any number of ways.

- "And then I started a ministry to help disabled people reenter the workforce."

- "And then I started my own business turning junk into art and now have twelve employees."

- "And then I met my beautiful wife, who taught me to love again."

- "And then I went back to school and got my degree in engineering, and now I build bridges."

- "And then I trained and competed in para-athletic sports events."

There are a number of ways to complete that story, but I rarely hear the story finished or even that it is currently being worked on. The people telling those stories have gotten hit in the face with life's two-by-four and think that event would make interesting reading. But it usually doesn't.

Creating Your Own Magic

That's because so far, the story includes only the setup. There is no triumphant ending. Think of your life like a magic trick. The magician shows you a birdcage with a small parakeet fluttering about inside. That's your life as it was before tragedy struck. Then the magician makes a sudden move, the bird vanishes, and the cage collapses. Tragedy strikes, you get in a car wreck, you get divorced, your health fails.

At that point, is your magic trick complete? You've shown your audience something amazing. Tragedy has happened, a bird has disappeared, and a cage collapsed. Is the audience satisfied at that point? Do they clap yet? No, because the trick isn't complete. The bird has to be brought back. It is the unwritten rule, the unspoken contract that every audience knows. In order for your amazing story to be complete, you have to finish your magic trick.

"But Charles, you said there is no magic in this world." That's right. Not unless you create it. My purpose in writing this book is to help you complete your magic trick. Don't listen to the lie that tells you that only special people can overcome, achieve, and conquer. Everybody can, but not everyone will.

Why is that? Well, some people are still waiting for their fairy godmother to arrive. Other people think their story ended with their tragedy. Some people think their life is someone else's responsibility. Some people are just too comfortable to pick up a hammer and start building their success story.

Let me ask you a question—and think carefully about how you answer it because your answer will indicate how much you have learned in this book. Ready? Here it is: Which would you rather hold in your hand? The right tool to get the job done or a magic wand?

If your inclination was to reach for the wand because, after all, it's magic, and with one wave you could make everything in your life okay, then you need to turn back to page 1 in this book and start over. If anyone—a motivational speaker, a New Age author, a preacher, teacher, or a candlestick maker—tries to sell you anything that resembles a magic wand, run away!

And the fact that there is no magic shouldn't discourage you. In fact, it should be one of the more encouraging things you've read, because now that you know there is no magic, you don't have to wonder if you're one of the lucky ones. You don't need to hope that fate will smile on you. You don't need to waste money gambling. You don't need to wish upon a star, hope your lucky number is chosen, or wait for the phone to ring.

What do you need to do instead? Here's what I suggest.

- Choose what you want in your life. Grab hold of the steering wheel of choice and begin owning all your decisions.

- Envision what you want your life to be and where you want to go. Work at polishing your vision windshield so you can discover your purpose, determine your desires, and discern your tomorrow.

- Program your mind with uplifting and encouraging materials. Load your mental GPS with the proper programming so you can navigate around difficulty.

- Take action and become a doer. Hit the action accelerator and put your plans in motion.

- Resolve to learn from your failure. Pack your emergency roadside repair kit with a healthy perspective of failure so that when you encounter it, you can use those experiences to propel you forward.

- Watch, build, and repair your character. Relentlessly guard and fortify your character frame so it can withstand the rigors of the road.

- Dare to believe. Power your journey with the engine of belief by actively believing in yourself, the people around you, and the world in which you live.

Millions and millions of people are sitting in dark rooms right at this very minute. They are afraid of what's outside. They are afraid to move and afraid to stay still. They wait to be rescued or to die. God only knows which.

But every now and then, a few of them dare to wander outside. They get tired of the dark, leave their fear behind, and begin their growth journey. I wonder if you are one of those people who will venture forth? I'd like to believe you are. I'd like to believe I'll see you on the road to success. I'd like to think that I'll be sitting across from you at the victor's table, hearing your amazing story.

HERE'S A THOUGHT...

The right tool is better than the best magic wand.

I'll tell you what. Let's you and me make an appointment to both be there. To both earn our right to sit at the table with all our heroes. To laugh, cry, and celebrate as they tell their stories. And when it comes time to tell our own stories, to not have to hang our heads in shame, but be able to proudly proclaim that we attempted something extraordinary and thus have become extraordinary ourselves.

ACKNOWLEDGMENTS

I would like to thank my wife and best friend, Laura, for making this book possible. I wouldn't be doing what I am today without your encouragement, support, and advice. Thank you also for the countless hours you've spent over the years editing and proofreading all my articles and books. You are an amazing person, and I'm privileged to be part of your life.

Thanks to all the teachers who invested their time and energy in me. My first-grade teacher, Ms. Millet, hugged and kissed all the kids in her class at the end of the school day. I know that's taboo now, but I remember feeling a little bit more safe and secure because she did so. Mrs. Cribbs, my fifth-grade teacher, published my poem, "Oh, Doctor!" in the school newspaper. I was stunned and flattered that a teacher thought enough of my writing to put it in the school paper. I still have a copy of it in the attic.

My seventh-grade math teacher, Mrs. Patterson, recognized my efforts to improve my grades by including me within a select group of kids in a special visit to the Mississippi College computer lab to learn about computers. My junior high band teacher, Mr. Mullins, gave me a chance to play what might arguably be the coolest instrument in all of known history. He also graciously granted me permission to mention him in this book. I still use some of the performance tips he taught me all those years ago.

My high school band teacher, Mr. Howard Cohen, bought chrome-plated Slingerland tri-toms to spare me from playing the bass drum yet another season. My guitar instructor at the University of Southern Mississippi, Michael Johnson, introduced me to classical guitar and helped me believe I had what it took to succeed as a musician.

My business mentors also played an enormous role in my journey. James O'Neal, took me under his wing as a junior sales associate at the now-defunct Waldoff's in Hattiesburg, Mississippi. Even though we were competing for sales, he made me feel as though he was there to help me become a better salesman and customer-service provider for my customers. My former boss, Aaron Meyers, at the Tom James Company in Atlanta, taught me much of what I know about how to run a business. Even though I was one of the worst salesmen on the team, Aaron spent time with me, training me and investing in my success.

There were people in the literary profession who worked to make this book a reality. My literary agent and friend, Chip Macgregor, continues to walk me through the process. Bob Hawkins, LaRae Weikert, Gene Skinner, and all the wonderful folks at Harvest House Publishers allowed me the privilege of working with them.

I think it's also important to recognize the vast contribution of my parents, Fred and Gwen Marshall. Any ability I have to connect with people is due to their influence and example. It's hard not to agree with Tom Brokaw that theirs was truly the greatest generation.

ABOUT THE AUTHOR

How fitting that Charles Marshall's first employer, a neighbor who paid him a dollar for doing yard work, wound up telling the then-nine-year-old, "I think you like talking more than you like pulling weeds." More than four decades later, Charles still has that dollar today, framed in his office. And he still likes talking more than pulling weeds, only these days people gladly pay to hear him speak.

As with most routes to success, Charles' journey took a circuitous path before leading him to his current role as a humorous motivational speaker. He delivered papers when he was ten, worked in convenience and grocery stores in high school, and manned the local hospital snack bar as a college student. He jokingly refers to the latter as his short-lived health care-career working as a "snack technician." He left that job and became a top salesman for an upscale department store, delivering his first motivational speech to his coworkers, sharing his secrets to improving sales.

Subsequent jobs included outside sales selling custom clothes, inside sales and customer service for a cleaning-chemical company, a self-employed professional musician traveling the Southeast, and a stand-up comedian performing for audiences nationwide. In 1998, he released his first full-length stand-up comedy video, *Fully Animated*. When he wasn't working, he often spent time performing for the homeless and elderly.

In 2001 Charles founded M Power Resources, a company dedicated to providing growth resources and materials for individuals and businesses. His first motivational book, *Shattering the Glass Slipper: Destroying Fairy-tale Thinking Before It Destroys You*, was published a couple of years later. In the meantime, his comedy career continued to gain momentum, and he released his second stand-up video, *I'm Just Sayin'!*, in 2008, along with a compilation of his syndicated humor column, a book called *I'm Not Crazy, but I Might Be a Carrier*.

Charles continues to use his comedic skills to enliven and energize his corporate presentations today. His more than two decades of experience making audiences laugh, plus a unique ability to communicate effective business strategies and insight, keep his calendar full even in the toughest of economic times. He travels more than 100,000 miles each year to speak to Fortune 100 and 500 companies, civic groups, nonprofit organizations, and numerous associations.

Charles currently resides in the greater Atlanta area with his wife, two children, and Scrappy, his ferocious, man-eating shih tzu.

Other helpful resources by Charles Marshall

available www.charlesmarshall.net

Shattering the Glass Slipper

If you're tired of waiting for success, it's time you read Charles Marshall's debut personal development book, *Shattering the Glass Slipper: Destroying Fairy-Tale Thinking Before It Destroys You*. In this exciting and groundbreaking motivational book, Charles Marshall exposes the infection of fairy-tale thinking and provides a prescription for the cure. Tired of waiting for your ship to come in? Then grab a hammer and build a boat with *Shattering the Glass Slipper*!

I'm Not Crazy, but I Might Be a Carrier

While other humor books gently tickle the funny bone, this one grabs hold and squeezes until you're laughing so hard you're gasping for breath. *I'm Not Crazy, but I Might Be a Carrier* is a laugh-out-loud collection of 40 essays from humorous speaker Charles Marshall. Each essay segues into a powerful spiritual message that uplifts and encourages the reader. Marshall admits he may not be entirely sane, but it's working for him. His point is that in spite of all the craziness life throws at us, there is always humor and encouragement to be found

I'm Just Sayin'!

From exploring off-the-beaten-path relationship markets and new-parent talk to wisecracking about The Donald's hair, there are no holds barred in Charles Marshall's punch-packed comedy video, *I'm Just Sayin'!* Long before the standing ovation, viewers will see why Charles Marshall ranks among the hottest comedians performing today. Loaded with behind-the-scenes extras, never-done-before alternate endings, and what many consider some of the best improv ever captured on film, *I'm Just Sayin'!* proves to be the best bang for the comedic buck.

To learn more about Harvest House books and
to read sample chapters, log on to our website:

www.harvesthousepublishers.com

HARVEST HOUSE PUBLISHERS
EUGENE, OREGON